Norman Goodland's Book

of

MORNING STORIES

(As broadcast by the B.B.C.)

Cover transparency: Paul Carter

CW01496245

Published by Paul Cave Publications Ltd.,
74 Bedford Place, Southampton.

Printed by Brown and Son (Ringwood) Ltd.

9 780861 460465

Ma

©

Goodland

First Published May 1984
Reprinted October 1984
Reprinted August 1985
Reprinted June 1986
Reprinted February 1987
Reprinted February 1988
Reprinted February 1989

ISBN 0-86146-046-4

CONTENTS

Page

Anniversary 7
JANUARY MORNING, 1948 8
JACKIE 13
FEBRUARY MORNING, 1960 18

Bain't Yere! 22

MARCH MORNING, 1976 23
THE CHOIRMAN 29
APRIL MORNING, 1947 34

Beware Woolly Aphis! 40

MAY MORNING, 1976 41
VERNON 49
JUNE MORNING, 1972 53

The Shelley Mob 57

JULY MORNING, 1974 60
THE COUNTY LIMP 64
AUGUST MORNING, 1970 69

Country Character 73

SEPTEMBER MORNING, 1979 75
THE HOLE IN THE HEDGE 79
OCTOBER MORNING, 1976 83

Wasn't it Strange? 88

NOVEMBER MORNING, 1950 90
THE CHRISTMAS TREE 94
DECEMBER MORNING, 1950 99

TAILPIECE 101

MORNING STORIES

In this collection, I again bring you old friends.

Stanley Rowe, with whom I worked on the farm in the late 1940's and the 50's, first taught me 'how to go on', — and the correct use of the Hampshire Language! He and his wife now live in Romsey, and have just enjoyed their Golden Wedding Anniversary; so they're still going strong!

You again meet the late Charlie Vane, who worked on the next farm to Stanley, (there *was* a little bit of rivalry between them, just a touch!) and who understood the language just as well.

Both men contributed to the character 'Old Stan', — who was me; perhaps you remember I broadcast the views of the Hampshire farm worker in the language, on the old West Region Radio Magazine, 'The 'Farmer'. I shall be ever grateful for their help.

Again I tell you of my foster-parents, Frank and Harriet West and their son Leonard, the Hampshire thatching family who lived up at the then remote village of Baughurst, near Basingstoke.

But this time, I introduce you to my own parental family. And out of that list there is now only one left — Aunt Nora, the one who rode the belt-driven Douglas Motorcycle.

Other new characters are our next-door neighbour up at Baughurst, Mr Schammel the Wireless Man. There is the Choirman who lost his voice. The 'Shelley Mob' — I used to work on Will's Nurseries at the back of the Vyne at Ower, but you will among these again meet Old Man Bungey.

There are those mortal enemies, Sandy the navvy, and Tommo the roadman. And Amos the poacher, and Charlie the Keeper; not *mortal* enemies, but living fairly close to each other in a peculiar sort of love-hate situation!

There's a bit about modern Country Character, and about Ma, my late Mother-in-Law, one of the bravest and most valiant souls I have known.

But there are *other* new characters you may find just as delightful, as you follow them through the seasons; birds, animals, reptiles, even insects. With all the radio and television and films and the endless hosts of books about these — is there anything more to add?

I think so . . .

There is a big difference between living a life totally different from them, and then going out to study, watch, photograph, — and *living with them* year-in, year-out, as the old-time landsman, woodsman and riverman used to do. *Then* — you become as much a part of their world as they are of yours.

Opposite: The author in his study. (Photograph: Radio Times).

Then — when they know you never do them any harm, they let their hair down! You don't need a 'hide' and all the other fancy stuff to get near them when that happens, and let their hair down they certainly do!

The scene is again Hampshire. Partly up beyond Kingsclere at Baughurst near Basingstoke, — mostly the Test Valley. You can come on a complete journey down the Test, from its source to its mouth. And we make the occasional exploration deep into the New Forest.

Oddities — the Hampshire streams dry in winter, flowing in summer — why is that? Little-known beaches — *still* hidden away and little known! A few dashes of poetry. Not everything all about the past — there is a keen glance at what modern farming is doing to our habitat.

I called the collection "Morning Stories", because they are grouped about some stories, (I did quite a few more,) I wrote and broadcast from the old West Region B.B.C., for the B.B.C. series "MORNING STORY".

VERNON was broadcast in October 1956, followed by THE CHRISTMAS TREE in the next month. JACKIE and THE CHOIRMAN were broadcast in the January of 1957; THE COUNTY LIMP in February 1961, and HOLE IN THE HEDGE in the following June.

Each story is preceded and followed by a selection of morning sketches I have written for the Hampshire County Magazine, covering a period from 1948-1979. I am still the monthly diarist for this illustrated publication, and the dates of issue for each sketch you will find beside the titles.

Tucked in between are the 'funnies'. These are from my diary pieces which I now broadcast weekly on 'Radio Solent', and they are repeated twice on the Saturday mornings on 'Solent Today'.

And as usual, I have managed to turn-up a TAILPIECE!

Norman Goodland.

ANNIVERSARY

It was the sixtieth Anniversary of the B.B.C., Steve Panton, Programme Organiser of B.B.C.'s 'Radio Solent' said to me,

"Wouldn't it be nice if you could do a 'look back' for us. Say — a piece about your first contact with Radio."

I knew he was probably thinking about the old B.B.C. West Region Radio Magazine, 'The Farmer'. It was presented by the last of the 'Wessex Greats' — Ralph Wightman. I think Bob Waller was its first producer, followed by Jimmy Thorburn.

It went out about the time when farmers and farm workers should be home for lunch. But although it was a magazine especially for them, *everybody* became interested in it. It built-up a terrific following from both town and countryside throughout the West.

I joined it to put the Hampshire farm worker's point of view, once a month. I did this for about 17 years. I did it in the language, as 'Old Stan'. But it all came to an end as 'The Archers' got going — round about the 1950's.

But — my very *first* contact with Radio went back a good deal further than 'The Farmer'. So I think Steve was just a little surprised to get this . . .

It was 1923 — or thereabouts. Mr Schammel lived next-door. He wore a blue uniform and a cap with a shiny peak, and a white shirt and black tie. He was a happy-go-lucky sort of man. Always smiling. Foster-mother said that was because he was a sailor.

I don't remember now whether he was in the Royal or Merchant Navy. But he was very special — a star-turn in the village. Mother was very proud to have such a neighbour.

Mother kept on about a 'Wireless Officer.' It was all very confusing. For one thing, I had never seen the sea. It was a long way away, and you had to go on a bus to Basingstoke to catch a train to get to it — so Mother said. But I *had* seen a boat. There was a man standing in it with a long pole. It was near a rick where Father was thatching.

And what was a 'Wireless' . . .?

Mr Schammel had some funny things next door in yellow boxes. He would put big earphones on, and stare at them. He would turn knobs, and screw things up. Mother said he was listening. He could hear people talking in London — and that was further away than Basingstoke.

Then one day she said, "Would you like to hear Big Ben on the Wireless?"

Who was 'Big Ben'? *I* didn't know whether I wanted to hear him or not. But Mother said, so I went.

Mr Schammel was smiling. He held the earphones in his hands. They sat me on a stool in front of him and he said, "Let me put these earphones on — and *you'll* hear Big Ben."

They didn't fit, so he had to hold them. *I* couldn't hear anything. I felt shut-off. I couldn't turn my head. And Mother's face came down and she said, "Don't *jump* — when you yeres it!"

That did it! I let out a bawl of pure fear, and Mr Schammel took the earphones off.

"What you frightened for boy?" asked Mother. "There's nothing to be frightened on!"

But it was no good. And Big Ben, — whoever *he* was — had to do whatever he was going to do — without me listening!

JANUARY MORNING, 1948
Malt House Farm, Braishfield

Darkness returns to the cow-pen. It comes tumbling down from its tall-roof hiding-place. It announces the approach of what proves to be the 'clearing-up' shower.

The roof sheet-iron creaks briefly above it — then suddenly sends down a huge roar from end-to-end of the building. It engulfs all other sound. Calves move in their box as a silent motion picture. They kick-out like deer; run to huddle, wide-eyed, in the far corner. As I wash-down the floor, my cowpen brush sweeps soundless as rubber. The water-bucket gives no rattle, no sound as I move it.

Water appears at the same time, on the slope of the farmyard flags. It is an endlessly-moving, criss-cross sheet. Brown-headed blobs bounce out of it, like an army of tiny soldiers running endlessly in open order down to the gulley.

The roar goes on, intensifies, — stops.

Silence in the roof.

Silence in the box; the calves remain stock-still.

Then everything recovers itself. The calves breathe and rustle once more. The storm-thrush flings-out its defiance from the ash-tree's head. The sun bursts forth in a yellow glare, and is greeted by a loud "QUARK!" from the dairy.

Nice weather for ducks! But even *they* won't face a sudden empting of the heavens like that! They are out now, hurrying joyously to the gulley — for farmyard ducks, *any* time is Spring-time.

Excited bill-dabbling. Head-bobbing with bills held curiously horizontal. Up-and-down, up-and-down, bob, bob, bob. Bill-dabbling from side-to-side. Up-and-down, up-and-down, — dabble-dabble-dabble faster and faster.

The blue-green-necked, short-legged Drake with his saucy black curl in his tail, waddles towards them.

"Quark! Quark!" — bob-bob-bob faster still!

The Drake purrs and bobs in reply. A wantan hussey nearest him settles flat to the ground. She tucks in her feet, thrusts her neck and head stiffly forward. The Drake stumps round her, bobs twice, clumsily mounts. She obliges by twisting her tail-feathers oppositely to the way he twists his.

The encounter is brief; off he shuffles, quiet and content. But the hussey will have none of it. Round and round him she dances, trailing her bill from side to side, then enticingly back over her shoulder as he follows her down to the gulley. There, the bobbing and dabbling and quarking begins all over again.

Hens, — Rhode Island Red, — come out from under the stone-staddled granary. One wanders in at the cowpen door, — squat, homely dusty-feathered, red-faced. Apparantly in no hurry. She cocks a golden-yellow-eyed side-glance and clucks conversationally. Or maybe she is irritated to see me here.

Opposite: "The blue-green-necked, short-legged drake, waddles towards his lady-friend". (Photograph: James Smith)

Then, for fooling, she pecks at an imaginary grain of corn. She turns and goes out again.

I move further on down the cowpen out of her way. She — nonchalantly, — reappears, and vanishes in silence behind the mangers.

After a while, I peep carefully over the back of the mangers. There is her red comb, all but buried in hay. But I am spotted at once, and again fixed by a golden-yellow eye. Completely still — I know what she's thinking. "I will hang on to this egg like grim death — until you go!"

All right — I do! I know that presently, I shall hear a couple of half-strangled cries. I shall see her wandering out, even more red-faced, looking for water. Any dirty old puddle will do. She'll take a couple of sips, and a studied stroll back along the way she has come. Then, safely clear, — as she thinks, — and utterly convinced that all this pretence has been a complete success, she'll announce to the whole farmyard that she's done it again!

"Yuck-yuck-yuck-yuck-YUCKOO! Yuck-yuck-yuck-yuck-YUCKOO!"

And I shall search the hay for the cosy, warm-rounded hollow where, once more, clean and white and warm will lie — my breakfast!

Battery-eggs with runny whites and the merest taste on the tip of the tongue and artificially-coloured yolks? Bah . . .!

My wife Sylvia comes in from washing-up in the dairy.

"Haven't you finished?"

"Nearly."

"Shall I get another bucket of water?"

"No — it's all right. I shan't be long."

My last job will be to bring in the hay-bales, break them and scatter them along the mangers. No lumps — or it will be wasted. But cows often leave good hay for unfathomable reasons. Save it, and mix it with the next lot, — and they'll leave it again. I remember one old farm-worker saying to me, "They dun't like no fodder a cat nor dog ben led on!"

'Pipe-o'-baccy' time. We look through the back door at a little scene framed by walls of stacked bales. A muddy track between them leads to the tangle of the orchard hedge.

Black old alder stands there, branch-crowded with red-and-brown tight-thumbed catkins, and old cones gaping from last September.

It is seed-year for the ash; ragged hanging bundles of brown propellor-blades awaiting the Spring gales to send them spinning down clear of the parent tree. Fieldfare flocks straggle above with clumsy, staggering gait, grumbling as they go.

As we have dinner at night, we decide on a walk after breakfast. We take the old road to Eldon . . .

By Hall Place Farm, — I wonder where *that* name came from? — stands a line of grey-white, rugged-barked walnut trees. Butts fissured and age-plated, crowns in a long spread of heavy brown twigs, crowding the sky. Even from the lane we see in silhouette trunkated twig-stubs, from whence fell the green, astringent fruits last October, or were taken by furtive rook and crow. I remember Adrian's — my youngest's — wry face as he tried to remove the bitter flesh with his teeth, to get at the convoluted white nut inside. But the bitterness never seems to deter the crow family.

We pass under ancient oaks and grey-trunked beeches, scarred deeply by initials and love-tokens. Who carved them? How long ago? 'I LOVE MARTY'. Did they marry? Where are they now . . .?

Great beeches stand broad-footed and heavy-toed, reaching through

10

mast-husk and drifted rolled-parchment leaf-fall, with their enormous, spreading grip. Stabilising an unimagineable tonnage of timber spread above each root eighty feet into the sky; a weight increased by as much again in the winter and spring gales.

We find one grown at the rim of an old chalk pit. Its roots knotted into the quarry, making steps all up its wall. Clearly the pit has not been used since before all this growth began, — at least a hundred and fifty years or more. Was this where the material came from to build our old chalk-walled cottage? Who knows how to build a chalk wall today . . .?

There are dark yews; and off the chalk, enormous horse-chest-nuts with resin-sealed flower-buds at fingers'ends. Waiting for the March sun to melt the glue to release their huge leaf-spread and tall canelabra. Marvellous to think that they all lie in embryo in incredibly tiny folds within these sticky buds, waiting . . .

And off the chalk, sweet chestnuts, too. Grey barks scored by great fissures up and down, with a twist at the base of each, as if some giant has passed through and idly turned them as he went by. Entirely different from the *horse* — chestnut — which isn't a 'chestnut' at all.

Eldon's little deserted Church still stands. We go inside.

Oaken pews, grey with dust, limed by the owl. A black-stained, half-rotted hassock. Stained prayer-books, ant-bitten and fly-marked. Webs weighted with dust, like curtains in dark corners. Even the altar-cloth still laid but hanging in rotting folds.

A place where God has long since been deserted. Where He himself grew tired of waiting, and so, has gone away. There is nothing of His Spirit here now. Only cool, regretful stares from simple, grubby-paned windows.

But it brings back memories. I had foster-parents, but eventually lived with my Grandparents and Aunts two miles away at the next village of Timsbury, when I was a boy. Sometimes on a Sunday morning, my Grandmother, Aunt Minnie and myself took the long footpath through the woods and up past Bill Pike the Keeper's cottage, to Eldon Church, — which wound on all the way to Winchester. Hurrying as we approached and heard the summoning bell rung, not from a tower, but from the branch of an apple-tree outside . . .

We return across the fields. There is little grass for the cows. And stretched out behind us is the long, shadowed bulk of the woods, like some huge dragon lying across the hills with oak and ash fungi silhouetted on his black back, his bramble snout overhanging the edge of the vale. Spouting blue clouds at the opposite thorn-tree goblin. Who cocks back his snook with his thousand woody fingers.

Frank West — "Father" in the story ("Jackie") — with his grandson, Michael Harvey, now master-baker at Ashford Hill, Kingsclere.

JACKIE

Foster-father's Workshop . . .

It fascinated me very much.

You came out into the little backyard. You went past the sandstone grindstone. Past the white-washed privvy under the yew tree — and there it stood: tall, dim, cool. Cobwebby. With a mixture of dried-dust and tarry smells, lingering round the door. And at angles and in odd corners all round the corrugated-iron walls inside, Father's thatching-tools, leaning. Curious. Gleaming softly, in the dusk.

Jackie lived in there. Up above the loft. In the dark . . .

When I looked in, I would hear his little scuffle. I would see his eye, gleaming. He'd bump along to the edge, and peer down with his head all cocked on one side. And he'd say,

"Chaak! Chaak!"

He didn't fly away. At first he couldn't; because Father 'nobbled' him as he said, — as he did the bantams. He clipped one wing so that if he tried to fly, he simply went round in circles.

He only did this two or three times as the feathers grew. By then, he had settled, and made the loft his home.

But Jackie was a thief. Nothing small or bright could be left where he could get at it. He hoarded most of it up in the loft, but some of it he dropped, and it would be lost.

So Foster-mother did not like him.

He would sit on anyone's shoulder, — except Mother's. And one day, he added grievously to his sins. He was on *my* shoulder. And suddenly, he started pecking at my eye.

He was very persistent about it. And I couldn't get him off. It frightened me, and I ran bawling into the scullery.

Mother was horrified. She knocked him from my shoulder, and he sprawled on the scullery floor. But with incredible impudence, he picked himself up and returned to the attack.

She seized the broom. There was a lot of screaming and bawling and fluttering; but eventually she settled his hash, and he hopped off back to the workshop to hide himself in his loft.

Mother looked at my eye, and bathed it. When Father came home, she shewed him the scratches. And she said,

"That vicious, *brute* of a bird! That boy could ha' been blinded!"

But Father said, "Tain't *viciousness'* Mother! 'Tis the *eye!* 'E goes for 't 'cause 'tis bright!"

But she said "Well *this* time — he *really will* 'ave to go!"

She had said this many times before, — but he didn't go . . .

Soon after Father had finished his tea, it was my bed-time. I changed before the red glow of the grate, and climbed up on his knee in my 'nightee'. He took his pipe out of his mouth and placed it on the mantel-shelf. Then he took my hands in his, and jigged me up-and-down . . .

"Bumpitty-bumpitty-bumpitty-bump — 'ere comes the gallopin' major . . ."

He sang the old song all the way through, and almost before he was finished I was saying, "gen!"

"Bumpitty-bumpitty-bumpitty-bump . . ." but he was now looking to see if Mother had lit the candle. She brought it in from the scullery.

"Right!" he said, and sat me on his shoulders.

Mother went ahead. "You *spiles* that boy!"

Up the steep, narrow stairs — "'Old tight! Mind yer 'head!" — and into the bedroom opposite theirs. Through the door with its angle cut off to fit the sloping roof, — and into the big bed with its brass nobs, its head against the central chimney-stack which divided our side of Wests' Cottages as they were called, from next door. A joyous tumble-in and tickling kiss from under Father's moustache, and a gentle "Goodnight! Say your prayers and be a good boy!"

I sat up and said them with Mother as he creaked off down again. Then she, too, kissed me 'Goodnight' and I watched her go out with the candle, and half-close the door . . .

A curious, distorted photograph of the little bedroom window appeared on the slope of the ceiling by the door. It travelled the length of the room and then disappeared by the chimney-stack. I knew it was because a motor-car was ambling its way down through the village with its lights on — Father had told me so when I first noticed it. But I could never figure-out where the photograph went when it disappeared . . .

When I came down in the morning, Mother was on her knees with dustpan and brush, sweeping the carpet. She wanted me out of the way. She left dustpan and brush on the floor and got up to put on my coat and scarf, gloves, red woolly hat, and 'Wellies'.

"Go out to play", she said. "I'll call you in for breakfast."

So off I went. Straight to the workshop — I had forgiven Jackie already.

I peered into the gloom. I called "Jack! Jack!" But there was no flutter. No bump. Nor any answer.

I called again. But the inside of the workshop remained — silent.

Sometimes, Jackie scrabbled about in the ditch. Or sat in the willow-tree. He *could* be on the copper-lid, down in the wash-house. Or strutting about on the garden path.

But — he was nowhere to be found . . .

I ran to into Mother and said "Mum! Jackie's gone!" She said "Yes I know he has. 'E's gone off to live with all the other jackdaws!"

I couldn't believe her. She said,

"He'll be much more happy, boy, livin' wi' they! He don't want to be all on 'is own — stuck up in that old loft!"

I could't see that. Jackie and I — we had endless games together! I was in tears. I said,

"It's Daddy's fault! He didn't clip his wing!"

Then she told me the truth. Before I was up, Father had pinned Jackie into his rush basket, put him on a pole over his shoulder, and gone off up to his thatching at Kimbrey's barn at the top of the Moor. There was a Rookery up there. He was going to let him go so that he could join the winter flocks.

I would not eat my breakfast. I spent the whole day grieving. And when I went to bed again, after prayers I said to Mother,

"Can I ask God to make Jackie good, and send him back home?"

She said "No! I shouldn't do that! You just ask Him to look after him and make him happy — where 'e is!"

She kissed me Goodnight. She pulled-to the white bedroom door quietly behind her. This time she left the candle high up on the chimney-breast.

It cast long, sad shadows. I worried and worried about Jackie. Eventually, I fell asleep . . .

I was awake at dawn. Nobody was up. Had Jackie come back . . .?

I got out of bed and crept downstairs. Light filtered dimly through the living-room curtains. My clothes were still in the armchair beside the fireplace. I could dress myself — with a struggle. I did so.

My coat was on a peg at the back of the scullery door. By straining on tip-toe, I could just reach it. I pulled, and down it came. I got it on — but I couldn't manage the buttons.

I struggled into my Wellies. But I couldn't find my scarf, my hat, or my gloves.

Again straining on tip-toe, I could just reach the leather thong which pulled-up the wooden latch of the back door. It shot up with a 'Bang!' The door was not bolted; deep in the countryside, it was not necessary in those days.

I pushed it open, and out into the yard I ran. Past the great sandstone grindstone. Past the privvy under the yew hedge. And into the workshop.

It was completely black. I called, softly, towards the loft. There was no answer. I called again. And I knew that Jackie was not there.

In the tops of the elms at the back of the Moor, there was huge activity and noise and bustle, all framed by the yellow fire of sunrise. I could see the comings and goings of rooks and jackdaws. I knew, — because Mother had said, — that Jackie was up there. So: if I went up and called him, he would come and sit on my shoulder. And then I could bring him home.

I crossed the plank bridge over the ditch, which led into the Moor. Frost peeped from between dark trees. It lay white upon the Moor. My hands began to feel cold. So did my feet. But I went on.

The rooks and jackdaws continued with their enormous conversation. I came up with the ploughland, and kept my course towards them.

From odd points of the field, there were irridescent glints; blue-black, gold, an occasional violet-green. They worried me — until I suddenly saw what they were. A slow, creeping host of silent birds, working the earth in the same direction, each following another.

The nearest studied my approach. Then it gave a kind of "Phwee!" and rose, flapping away from me, into the air.

Like magic, the rest rose together in a screaming multitude. Up, up in a great circling mass, higher and higher. Sunlight searched-out their white underparts. I gazed in wonder as each of the host flickered black-and-white, black-and-white. They revolved in a vast, winking cloud, edging away, slowly circling all the time.

The ploughlands were hard-frozen, so I plodded on. I was now faced by the chorus of rooks and jackdaws; rough, brash, loud. Shouting in the burning glare of the rising sun.

My approach was ill-received. When it became clear as to where I was heading, a vast silence descended.

I stood still. I looked and looked — for Jackie. But there were so many of them there. I called "Jack! Jack! Come on Jackie! Come home!"

The answer was a huge, unnerving roar from the elm tops. Hoarse voices, some high, some low, with the irritable "Chack! Chack! Chack!" of jackdaws intermingled.

Plucking up courage, I moved a little closer. The long, warning "Caws" changed to irritable and angry barking. And then, with a thunder of wings the whole Rookery citizenry took-off in a vast, cumbersome exodus across the sky. The coppice trees blanketed their voices except for the continued

15

jackdaws' "Chaak-chaak-chaak!"

I was very uncertain as to whether to go back home, or go on. I could see the cottage away down the Moor, and still felt safe. But I decided to have one more try. There was a ride before me, into the coppice, which led-out to the other side. I entered into it, and the cottage was gone . . .

Years later, I learned from my Foster-parents what happened meanwhile. When Mother got up, she glanced into my bedroom. She saw the bed empty. Not particularly bothered, she went downstairs. But I was not there either.

She called out to Father, who was shaving in the scullery,

"Where's the boy?"

"I dunno," he said. "Isn't he upstairs?"

"No!" said Mother. "He isn't!"

So Father said, "P'raps he's out on the privvy!"

Mother bustled out to see. Nobody on the privvy. She searched around, called, bustled back in.

"He's not *there!*" And she called through the house. And called again outside. And at last they both realised I was not at home.

Then Father said, "*I* know where he's gone!"

"Where then?"

"He's gone to find Jackie!"

"Well!" Mother said. "You best go and find *him!* Quick as you can! 'E'll be froze!"

She rushed back into the scullery and saw that at least my coat and Wellingtons were missing. She looked in the table drawer.

"He hasn't got 'is scarf nor 'is gloves! Not 'is 'at! For goodness' sake Father — hurry-up do!"

Father made his way up to the deserted Rookery. He stood in the empty coppice. He called. But of course, he got no answer.

He was pretty sure that I had followed the flock. Where, then, would it be?

From the bright hour of sunrise, the scene was changing. Clouds gathered in the sky in long, purple lines. There was the smell of dampness in the air. So Father knew the flock would not have gone far. They would be hanging around Hyden Hill, which they generally did on such days.

So he, too, came up through the ride. And out on the other side of the coppice — he spotted me. Far away, trying to find a hole in the tall hedge on this side of Hyden Hill . . .

I heard him call. I waited for him to come up, tramping along the same deep finishing-grip in the ploughlands that I had followed.

"What you up to — you young rascal!"

I told him I was looking for Jackie. He produced gloves and scarf and hat, and put them on. He said,

"You'd better come 'ome along wi' me!"

"But Jackie!" I said. "He's over there!" And pleaded with him to go and see.

Father gave in. We found a gap in the hedge. We could be the flock waddling and fussing in the field; probing, quarrelling, shovelling. They rose to move-off to a safer distance. All — except one.

Quite close to us, a bedraggled jackdaw stood miserably hunched. On the crest of a furrow.

16

"That's him! That's Jackie! Jack! Jack!" I called. I made to run towards him, but Father said, "Stay still, son!" And the jackdaw, bobbing from crest to crest, came to us.

I was very excited. "Come on Jackie — come on!" It flew up on to my shoulder. Father held out his hand. Jackie jumped on Father's finger and climbed up his arm. Then he hitched-in his claws on Father's shoulder, sinking down, exhausted. Father picked me up, and we began the journey home.

When we emerged from the coppice, he put me down. Mother was out beyond the hedge bordering our garden, looking. As we came down, she saw the bird perched on Father's shoulder. She was not pleased — but *I* was!

"He's back, Mummy! Jackie's come home!"

She said "Don't you never do nothing like this agen! You could ha' ben lost out in them fields! You could have frozen to death! You could ha' caught your death-o'-cold! Come on in in the warm!"

We crossed the plank bridge, Mother still glaring at the bird. It suddenly hopped off Father's shoulder, and ran gratefully to the shelter of the workshop. Back into the familiar loft. Father closed the door behind it . . .

When he came home that day from thatching, he had a bundle of withey-rods tied to his back. After tea, he lit his lantern and went out to the workshop.

I wondered and wondered what was going on. I pleaded to go out to see. But Mother said, "You're not going out to that ratty old place with that bird! Wait 'til your Father comes back!"

It was nearly bedtime when he did. And in his hand, he carried a large cage made from the withey-rods. With Jackie balancing on the perch inside, looking very ruffled, and extremely put-out!

"About time too!" said Mother. "Pity you 'adn't done it long ago! We wouldn't have been put to all this bother!" Then, as Father made for the stairs door, "Where you takin' it?"

"Up to the boy's bedroom!"

"Ho no you're not!"

Father said, firmly, "Just for the one night!"

Mother stiffened. But she did not say "No".

After she had put me to bed and I had said prayers, I asked her "Shall I say 'Thankyou' to God for helping us to find Jackie?"

"If you must," she said.

I gave thanks, and Mother kissed me Goodnight and settled me down. But the bird was wakeful until she came in later.

She thought I was asleep. I heard her whisper, "You needn't think you're going to stay *'ere! 'Cause you ain't!'*"

The feathers rose on the bird's neck. Mother blew-out the candle, and the moon smiled in. Jackie watched her go out of the bedroom.

Shadows and moonlight filled the room. Silence came. Jackie turned himself on his perch away from the moon. He squatted down, and tucked his head under his wing . . .

17

FEBRUARY MORNING, 1960
Eldon Lane off Lower Street, Braishfield

Daisies on the lawn. Only one or two — but they're there.

A periwinkle! Down in the shade almost on the ground — that little blue flower!

All up through the orchard floor, all under the shaggy old arms of the old apple-trees — a tangle of shadows. Couch-cushions bleached — but green at the stump already! Leaf-fall packed between, black with moisture. And snowdrops sheltered behind them, bowing their heads.

The lane wanders its way on up to the Downlands, just as it did in the horse-farming days and the ox-farming days before that. It lengthens the journey — but eases the slopes. It was easier on the horses, going up. And coming down, if the wagons and carts were heavy-laden, there was a better chance of dropping the braking shoe before the loads bore-down on the horses.

It's a deep lane with high banks, — very old. Perhaps when the soil was blown down off the hills, or washed-down by the rain, and it was all broad-leafed Forest where the fields are now, it began as an animal-track.

But the hedges down here aren't as old as that. They're hawthorn — 'May' as we say in the countryside. Planted. Perhaps in the farm-enclosure days.

Walk quietly. Talk *softly* . . .

There's a yellow bird high on that hawthorn branch at the far end of this next stretch! Just keep walking, keep talking, — he'll think we haven't *seen* him!

Oh he's spotted *us!* He said so — TCHICK! Who would think such a little bird could have such a loud voice? He's said it again — but not quite so loud this time!

It's all right — he thinks we're not interested! Up goes his head, beak open — can you see his little needle tongue? Throat puffed — ''Little-bit-of-bread-and-NO-cheese!''

No mistaking *him* — the Yellow Hammer. He'll sing on now right through to September.

You know you're near the Downs when you see him. He doesn't like the valley. He doesn't like the woods — or the trees. He's telling us we're on his patch. Got his eye on the hedge-bank already I shouldn't wonder, to set-up home. He won't go now — so long as you don't stare *too* hard!

That blackbird's not happy! Flitting about one side to the other . . .

He's unsettled the Yellow-Hammer. *There* it goes, bounding along between the hedges. Whirrs its wings — a bound — another whirr — gone — round the corner! And 'tac-tac-tac' to *you* Mr Blackbird! You frightened our Yellow Hammer away . . .!

Celandines in the ditch. So we're still on the claylands. See how they stare at the sun!

Hazel hedges now. The wands have grown out from the stumps where they used to cut and lay the hedges in days gone by. Sunlight in the catkins — like fool's gold! *(See the picture opposite).*

Dog's Mercury down there — just beginning to leaf! Primrose rosettes — and bluebell spears already! Rose briars — and a spindle-tree.

'Spindle'? Oh — they used to make spindles out of it because it's one of the hardest woods there are. For spinning-wheels.

Loads of bramble! Well it *is* Braishfield — Saxon for 'Bramblefield'.

This one is an *old* hedge, — *very* old. If you see primrose and bluebell and dog's mercury in a hedge — it's old. They grow normally in broad-leafed woodlands. So if you see them in a hedge, you know that hedge is all that is left from the Forest which once grew there, before Man started felling and farming.

But some of these old hedges were planted, too. You can guess the age of them by the dog's mercury growing in them.

Dog's mercury spreads, so the experts say, at about eight inches a year — well, it depends on whether it's facing the North or the warm winds from the South or West. So if the wood is still standing where it has spread from, you measure from there to where it stops in the hedge, and divide it by eight inches.

The experts have found hedges like that going back to Roman times. Some to Saxon or Celtic times — some prehistoric. A building or a monument as old as that, it would likely be preserved. But the farmer can come along and rip it out — just like that! He doesn't *know* you see! If he did know, — perhaps he wouldn't care. Especially if it was in the way of his modern machines.

We're nearly at the top. Let's go in through this gap . . .

You can see right down through the valley to the sea. Twenty years ago, I was hoeing in this field. Three of us; my wife, the farmer and me. That was before it was taken-in by the Estate . . .

We used to stand up to ease our backs and look away out to the sea. That end bit of the Isle of Wight jutting-out with the water gleaming in front of it I used to call 'The World's Corner'. You could see smoke pillars creeping round it on a still day from the steamships. If they grew larger and larger you knew the ships were creeping in to Southampton Water. If they became smaller, you knew the ships were creeping out to sea.

A farm is a bit like a garden; — well it was in those days, there was so much work to be done by hand, — you can become a prisoner to it. I used to think how marvellous it would be to be on one of those ships — sailing away. Free from the cycle of work, year after year after year, of the land . . .

Let's stand behind this bramble-hill. The field-birds won't spot our white faces.

There's still some big elms down there free of the disease. All pink in the crown — that's the flowers.

There's a bird gone up from furrow! Up it goes round and round and round, gliding, shaking its wings with song! Every time its song bursts out it goes a bit higher — and a bit higher . . .!

Oh! End of performance! Down like a stone! You'd think it would crash to the ground but no; it spreads, glides-in, runs a bit and there it is walking. Slowly, sedately. Crest up — can you see? The skylark, of course.

Why did it drop? Well it's cold up there — there's a low stream of damp air. Dropping suddenly like that before they're properly up, — that's one of the ways country people know it's going to rain.

The old cock-partridge has seen us, brambles or no brambles! Out *there* look — that stumpy little fellow on the furrow-top, like a little soldier! Head up — watching!

He's *bold* just along now. He's courting. Look two or three yards behind him — can you focus your eye on that little brown hump? *That's* his girl-friend! Tail down, head down, trying to look like a clod! Watching *him* —

while he watches *us!*

He's off — the hen after him! Right up the furrow, right up to the end — under the barbed wire — gone! Into the corn-chimps and down the other side of the slope!

Don't move! There's a *butterfly* — just one! A bit ragged and faded! Wintered in a tree-hole or behind some loose bark I shouldn't wonder!

There — it's found a sun-spot! It spreads, soaking-up the sun!

It *is* faded — but you can see what it is! Yellow-and-black forewings with a dark edge. 'Eyes' just faintly marked on the outer corners. Two more, darker, on the lower wings all rusty-brown! It's a Peacock.

Don't show yourself! Look out to the middle of that fallow . . .

See anything moving? White smudges and gleams — see that? That flash of green right in the middle of them — yes, you've got it! Black-and-white plovers. Pee-whits in their cocked hats!

Inch-by-inch, foot-by-foot, they'll work right through the stubble all day if it's fine. All through the countryside, plovers shift hundreds of *tons* of wireworms, larvae — all sorts of pests from the fields!

Listen — there's one fluting! Up he goes — round and round like a mad thing! Fluting again and now down — down — down — this way that way — a power dive! Split-second stall — wings out, tail spread — a lung-compressed PHEE — OO — WHIT! — a run forward, feathers up, crest cocked high!

So what was all *that* about? It's his challenge — it's nearly mating-time!

The cows are out from milking. Coming out from behind the stack and the farmyard roofs, all gleaming in the sun. Not very willing — from their warm cowpen.

There's the old dairyman, shoving the last bunch on through. He's got a struggle there —closing that five-barred gate against the mud! They'll move-on — the mire is cold to the hoof. They'll get on the pasture when they get fed-up with it — where it's warmer.

A *pheasant* — hear him? *Funny* call, isn't it? Always reminds me of somebody tapping a cracked jug in the middle of the woods!

A fool of a bird! Pheasants wouldn't survive if they didn't have a keeper to look after them — and keep them alive to be shot!

You can take a pheasant off his roost as easy as winkie — if you know where and you know how! I'd better not tell you that! The fool always tells you *exactly* where he's roosting! He clatters his wings and gives his old cracked-jug call just where he's going to settle down! Any poacher or farm-hand on his way home will make a mental note of an idiot announcement like that!

We'd better go. There's the storm-cock sitting in the tree-top like a jewel, pouring-out his song . . .

We'll come up this lane one *evening*. We might see the bat-mouse. It catches insects and eats them as it flies; up the lane, down the lane and up the lane again, between the hedges. You don't hear him fly — his wings are noiseless, like an owl's.

Stand still long enough for him to come back, and as he comes towards you he may glide, perhaps no higher than your shoulder. If he does that, when he passes he'll pass on a line exactly mid-way between you and the bank. He's got a built-in 'sonar' you see . . .

And if your ear is keen enough, you might *just* catch a thin little 'chirrup'. And *that's* his *base* note . . .!

Bain't Yere

"She bain't yere!"

The Head Dairyman is a black shadow, silhouetted. Leaning, over the half-door of the milking-bail.

He has sent me out in the rain to fetch the cows. *Fifty* of them. Ayreshires. And there he is, in the dry, surveying the floodlit holding-yard.

How on earth does he know there is *one missing* — from all this lot?

"No!" he says again, "She bain't yere!"

"*Who* bain't yere?"

"Why — old Milly! Same old hedge-hanger as yesterday! I'd a-thought you'd looked out vor 'er! You'll ha't' go back and' fetch 'er!"

There seems something between a sneer and a grin on his face. The rain hisses down . . .

Back up the hill in the gloom. Past the woods, with rain scattering off trunks in the torchlight beam, like steel splinters in a shower. Leaf-fall starts-up to its downpour.

I push open the gate leading into Far Field, and begin the search. A few old cow-flops lead-off round the corner of a wet bramble-hill. I follow them round.

I am looking up into a sort of cavern beneath the elms. And my torchlight suddenly illumines — old Milly's swollen udder, and tall backside!

I am not happy.

"Come *out* — you old bleeder you . . .!"

Old Milly charges on through . . .

I don't make the same mistake the following morning. Hedge-hangers always 'hang' in the same place. So I go there first. And there she is again. And *out* she comes . . .!

The herd sail and rock their hulks through the gloom, following the boss cow down through Far Field gate. And on down towards the floodlight, poised like a distant star above an ocean of mud. They coast-in and drop anchor in the holding-yard again.

I've just about made it. Heavy drops begin to thud down from the black cavern of the sky . . .

The Head Dairyman is *again* a silhouette. In the dry, leaning over the half-door. And once again I hear the hated cry —

"She bain't yere!"

Ah — the old fool's *wrong* this time!

"Ho tes she ruddy-well is! I hucker *'er* out *first!*"

"'Ucked *'oo* out first?"

"Old Milly o' course!"

"Oh *she!* Tain't *she* — *she's* yere! 'Tis *Edith! She* bain't yere!"

Once more that sneering grin spreads across his face.

"You'll ha' t' go and fetch 'er! And you'll ha' t' get a *move*-on! Else we shain't get the milk out on time!"

And as if to underline his point, the heavens open — and the rain *hisses* down . . .!

MARCH MORNING, 1976

The Winsor, Copythorne, Ower are when it was still part of the New Forest, and there was no motor-way, and the Farmer had not ploughed up what was left.

Rabbit-runs . . .

They don't 'run' really. They hop. In a *fresh* run you'd see little depressions in the grass, something under a foot apart. But if it's a run in constant use it doesn't look much different from any other small-animal run.

Pony-tracks, meandering through the gorse . . .

And they don't *really* meander . . .

Bert Taylor was a Commoner. He had rights to run ponies, cattle, donkeys, — even pigs at certain times of the year, — on the New Forest on free range. He told me that animals on free range *don't* aimlessly wander. He said they form or join herds. And the herd behaves much as if it was in the wild — which of course it is.

He said they have their own regular routes to their feed, or to water, or to shelter. Feed varies according to seasons — so will the route. It varies according to the wind, too; cattle tend to feed into the wind but travel away from it. I think he said it is the other way round for ponies — but I wouldn't be sure of that.

Anyway, he said if you know all these things you can pretty-well tell where your animals will be at any time. Which is especially useful if you have a free-range milking herd, because when there is plenty of feed growing in the Forest, you might have to go out and bring them in for milking.

Here's an old ride — or it *might* be an old lane. All fresh and green with soft-grass. All undisturbed. But you need your Wellingtons. Because in winter and early spring it becomes a catchment-area for surface-water. Inches deep in saturated leaf-fall.

Never mind — we'll splosh on. Marvellous — green life sprouting from those tough old bramble-skins already!

There's a dry stretch here. Pebbles pressed hard into white sand . . .

The little brook running beside those laurels almost disappears in the summer — but it swells with each passing shower. That's because we're on clay — the rain can't soak away.

More grass — and the brook crosses the ride, — and off down the slope. If you look — you'll see the grass it flows over is all swept the same way by the current. There's humus and leaf-mould pressed up against its roots. The grass in the water is longer, stouter and greener than in the rest of the track.

That's where they got the idea from — of water-meadows. The drowners — the men who look after water-meadows, — flood and drain-off at intervals, from the river. They start that in late February and March and might do it again in the autumn.

The idea is that the water protects the grass from the cold, and the flooding spreads humus and silt carried-down by the river, — and chemicals especially in the chalk-lands. You don't have to cultivate or fertilise — the river does it all. But the drowners do have to look after the flooding and draining system.

Let's follow the brook. Away it goes — under the wiry stems of heather. The heather flowers are still on the bushes from the summer — like tiny bleached-out skulls. Green shoots already — the ponies will be after them.

Here's where it ends. In a water-bog. Clear brown —right down to the humus . . .

I've heard it said that Forest brooks are brown because of iron in the soil. I don't know about that. If you pick-up a brown leaf from the Forest floor in autumn on a damp or foggy day and turn it over, — you'll see little globules of moisture on the back — all stained brown. If you crush it between your finger-and-thumb, you'll get brown stain on your fingers. So it could be decomposed chlorophyl that stains the water. Whether there's any iron or not in *that,* — I don't know.

Anyway, there's plenty of leaf-fall down in there. Stir the humus with your toe. *There* look — pine needles, oak leaves, beech, bramble, hawthorn leaves and leaf skeletons and stems — all floating out. Some bleached white, some brown, most black. The beginnings of peat, and the beginnings of coal you see.

This is 'Forest' too, — although it's moor, acid and musty. Rank on rank of tussock-grass. Some of those tufts are ages-old. Two or three feet tall, and top-heavy. You can cut your fingers on that grass — even when it's bleached. A lot of them covered in moss . . .

Come on — but be careful! Test each tuft before you put your weight on it — because some of them will topple. We'll make for those knolls leading across to the other side . . .

Only scraps of Scots Pine on the knolls. Huddled, stunted, crooked, rough-headed — they don't stand much chance here. The soil's too bitter, and they've no shelter. But — it's a start! Things *do* grow. The water gradually gets soaked-up, and the big trees come later. But not in *our* time! Nor our grand-childrens', either!

There we are — through! Holly-bushes and rhodedendrons ahead. They make a marvellous wind-break with those leathery old leaves — but they do spread so. A few logs, — barks all gone, white and polished by the weather.

A sun trap! We'll sit on a log for a while. If we keep still — we might see something . . .!

There . . .*!* Don't *move* . . .*!* On that far log — a doe-rabbit . . .!

How do I know it's a doe? Because of her slender little head. A buck-rabbit's head isn't as slender as that.

She's cocking — and listening! One ear turned towards us! Speak softly . . .!

Now she's scanning. Keep still — and we'll just be apart of the furniture! She's scanning with her other eye on the other side, just as carefully!

Well-fed — you can see the folds of her nape gleaming in the sun. Been at the gorse-shoots I expect! Perhaps she's from a January litter — or last month's. Oh — they're grown-up within a month or so and looking for a mate!

Scratching under her ear — I expect she's full of fleas! Showing her powder-puff, — that's her signal to the others — "I'm here!" Useful in the dusk or at dawn, but the trouble is other things know the signal too!

We *say* 'rabbits' — but properly speaking, they're 'conies'. A *rabbit* is a young,or baby coney.

Quite a barrier — the rhodedendrons! Plenty of green flower-buds. Tough, elongated, — leathery, like the leaves. See how polished they are, —

Pigs in the New Forest — Thorn's Inclosure. (Phtograph: Robin Fletcher)

how they reflect the sun! Green mirrors — like you see in the holly!

Well — if we can't get through — its a hands-and-knees job — under! I've done this before. I'll break the way — you follow.

Passageways you see — full of dead tangle. It's all brittle — it breaks at a touch. It's the skeletons of border-twigs, when the bushes were small. Then when they grew up and touched each other over the top, these twigs underneath were starved of light and just died off.

Like a brown feather-bed the leaf-fall — you could sleep on it! Quite dry, considering. Warm to the knees and hands.

I found this secret world when I was a boy. The black, blue-green, yellow-green canopy. Like a stained-glass dome here, with the light filtering through. And sun-spots on the leaf-fall — they look bright enough to blaze-up and catch it on fire!

Hold on — we'd better stop! There's a ground-movement just up there — very slight . . .

Wait . . .!

Ah! There he goes — quietly sliding out — the Viper! Beautiful! Olive-green, — black zig-zags down his back! He's sluggish because he hasn't long crept out from his winter hole.

He heard us crashing through the twigs. He's confused I expect, because he wouldn't be able to tell in here where it came from. So he watches — with his copper-red eye.

Don't worry. He won't attack. He's just anxious to creep away into his gloom. So we'll give him plenty of time to go . . .

Adders *are* beautiful creatures, — but they're not all the same. Some have *diamonds* down their backs and they can be dark or light brown, instead of olive. They can be grey to nearly white with brown diamonds. Or so dark, you can't see the markings at all.

If you get bitten — it's serious. Snake-catchers like old Brusher Mills, gypsies and such will quickly slash a cross on the bite and suck-out the blood and spit it out to stop the poison getting into the system. It might work. But whether you can do that or not — it's off to the nearest hospital in double-quick time!

They are not actually aggressive. They only attack if you frighten them — or tread on them. You can easily do that if they're coiled-up on a pebbly bank in the sun, asleep. With markings like that you need a keen eye to pick them out — if they're still. The best thing if you're out on the moorland in Spring or Summer or on into Autumn, is to wear Wellington boots or boots and gaiters. And always have a careful look-round before you sit down.

Anyway, if you're not creeping about and the children are making their usual noise — they'll *hear* you — and they won't be there. People don't *often* get bitten . . .

He's gone! Keep an eye — and we'll press on . . .

That's it — we can stand up now! Birch-stems — all agleam. Pink-fleshed under horizontal strips, with silver-wash skin all peeled away. No leaves as yet . . .

Look up there! Traceries against blue sky! And the big, sleepy green-black towers of Corsican Pine staring down on it all . . .!

Moss now — everywhere. All the shades imagineable! Bright yellow, green, brown, green deeper even than the rhodedendrons. Look — there's sort of *feathers* growing out of that patch there — just like a miniature fir plantation! Another forest, you see, for all the squirmies waking up for the Spring underneath.

"New Forest ponies don't aimlessly wander. They have regular routes to regular feeding places". (Photograph: Robin Fletcher)

Here are the pine-trees — rank on rank. Scaly old barks with the sky all pale-blue between. Look-out for the needle-fall on the pebbles! It turns the slopes into glissades!

You can smell spiced resin — and listen! A web of tiny voices up there — tysing, sii-ing! Siskins and other tiny birds searching the buds and young cones.

There's the cruel old white-and-vinegar-brown jay with his black tail and his black moustache and his crest up! Away he bounds from cover to cover! One of the most beautiful birds you'll see with his blue-and-white barred shoulders and his chestnut wings.

Beautiful language, too! He curses us to damnation as he goes . . .!

Nor has he beautiful habits — he's an egg and fledging thief. I remember old Percy the Gamekeeper when I was a boy, and he said, *"Juggers* jays is, you know! If you got an old 'en wi' chicks runnen round — 'e'll be arter 'em — depend upon that! And they gets arter the pheasant-chicks, too!

"And I'll tell thee another thing about they jays! If you 'appens near 'is nest in the Forest, 'e'll set right up on timber-top and screech unearthly!"

We've startled the Yaffle — the Green Woodpecker! There he goes, red and white and green and a glimpse of his yellow backside — bounding along through the echo of his own laughter . . .!

What a commotion! But all the time that web of little voices up above still goes on, undisturbed . . .

Beeches now, — with long spindle fingers sweeping almost to the ground. Plenty of light under them this time of year — but in couple of months the canopy will be so dense practically nothing will grow under them! The frost has curled the leaf-fall like little yellow parchment-rolls. In drifts so dry, so light — they whisper and float and roll at the merest brush of the foot . . .!

Birches again — and here's the lane leading back to Ower. They haven't trimmed the thickset this winter, so it's all untidy. But it suits that butterfly — a yellow-green Brimstone. Swooping, diving. Fluttering along by the hawthorn and the spindleberry and the briar. Stopping here — fluttering there — then up over the other side. Looking for buckthorn I expect, to lay her eggs on its leaves. Far too early — they don't leaf until next month.

Will's Nurseries! I worked on them when I was a young man. The old pump-house is still there. And the pool beside it where they used to pump-out water for the greenhouses. Let's go and have a look — no one will mind . . .!

A funny old upright pumping-engine — they haven't used *that* for some time by the looks of it! An old Diesel I think. They used to start it with a blow-lamp. I can't quite remember whether they used just to heat the top of the cylinder — or stick something in the top and heat it. Anyhow — when they'd got it hot you stuck a handle in the fly-wheel and spun it like mad and then — chug-chug-chug-chug — it got started!

Look into the pool! That's *toads!* Males locked about the females — A batrachian orgy! *Two* locked round one — *three* round another! She's all white and dead — entrails squeezed out of her mouth — horrible!

We used to prize them apart sometimes — and they'd go straight back again. And there's chains of jelly with eggs in them like double rows of little black beads — floating just underneath look, and wound round every water-plant in sight.

Listen . . .!

Can you hear croaking coming up from the bottom through the water? Who says toads don't croak? And how do they do it — down in there — where there's no air?

Toads, they say, always come back to the pond where they first saw light of day, for this breeding-orgy.

Think about that . . .!

If it's *true* — there should only be only one original pond where the toads all came from in the first place, — for them to go back to! So how did they spread to the others . . .?

That's a puzzler — isn't it? We'll figure it out on the way home . . .!

28

THE CHOIR MAN

'Course you know — one time, old *Charl* was a bit of a beggar for 'is 'ops! Oh I knows 'e's a Pillar of the Church and all that, — but 'tis *true!*

You see — when he'd spent a day bumpin' they hurdles in the coppice, 'e'd draw on in to the Wellington Arms on 'is way 'ome, just "t' lay the doost in me throat," as 'e used to say. Always for "a quick -un", an 'ad "to get back *early* tonight," and all that — but he was gen'lly amongst the last, come chuck-out time.

Well — beer never made un drunk, so much as it made un *sing!* But the funny thing was , 'e never used to sing in the pub! No 'twas after 'e'd got 'is old bicycle out from the pub woodshed, and gone on up Wellington Hill that he used to start!

And by gum — *didn't* 'e start! 'E 'ad a voice like a steam-argen as you could yere through the valley from one end to t'other!

And it always went this way. When 'e'd jes left the pub, some o' they songs 'e was trollen' out there — well they wasn't very *respectable* — like! And if you was walkin' wi' your Missis or somebody like that — well you trudged along wi' yer ead down and you pretended you couldn't *yere* it!

But then 'e drawed on up by old Mary Dimmity's there — a proper old spinster gal as got no time for men nor never been kissed b' one in 'er life I shouldn't wonder, — 'e used to change to love-songs. Old 'uns o' years gone by! "Come into the Garden Maud." "The Old Rustic Bridge by the Mill" — and stuff like that.

Then up by the Colonel's 't'd be old Boer War songs — "We dun't want t' fight but b' jingo if we do — we got the guns, we got the men, we got the money too!"

And do you know — when 'e was singin' *sensible,* — 'is voice used to troll out up along the brickworks there and come down acrost the fields real *beautiful!* I s'pose when you come to look at it, wi' 'im bein' on 'is own like 'e was wi' they 'urdles year in, year out, 'e sart o' *trained* 'is voice to echo like it would in the open spaces. Ya — when 'e got on to they old songs our Feythers used to sing years gone by — 't'd be really *enjiyed!*

But when 'e got a bit further alongside th'old Vicarage — oh dear oh dear! 'E'd come over all religious! 'E'd bide on the verge by the Post Office and lean over 'is bike lookin' straight up at the Vicarage windows, and gie the old Vicar a few tunes in 'is own line. "All things Bright and Beautiful"! "We Ploughs the Fields and Scatters"! Or if 'twas about Christmas time "Whiles Shepherds watch their Flocks by Night" — and stuff like that! And tere 'e'd abide until the lights come up in the Vicar's bedroom — and 'e'd gie un jes one more for luck — and away 'e'd go!

Well — we knew *that* couldn't go on for ever! We knew it 'cause the old Vicar 'd sort of half complained about it like, when 'e went over the Post Office t' git 'is papers — and o' course it got round!

Any'ow — one night old Charl was down at the Wellington with the rest of us and he says,

"What's think you? The old Vicar 've asked I to jine the *Choir!*"

"Jine the *Choir?*" we says. "'Ow come that then?"

"Waal," Charl says. "I were up in coppice there bumpin' me old 'urdles and when I looked up — blow me if the old Vicar wadn't stood there! So — you know, bein' polite-like, — I stopped, and I says to un 'Good Mornin' Vicar!' And he says, 'Good mornin'! Not singing today then, Charlie?'

"So I says to un 'I didn't see thee comen — or I'd ha' gie thee a tune! Hi'll gie thee one *now* if thee likes!"

"No need to!" he says. "I've heard you singin' outside the Vicarage on a number of occasions now! And do you know what I've come up here for?"

"I thought 'Oh dear — *now* we're going to 'ear summat!' But do you know what 'e said? 'E said 'I've come up to tell you, Charlie, how much I appreciate that *beautiful* voice of yours! Singing those hymns in the darkness on top of the valley at *eleven o' clock at night* and sometimes *later,* — and to say that it sounds really lovely!'"

"Well," we says "It *do* Charl! It *do!*"

"And then 'e says 'A bit *disturbing* mind, when you have to wake up and switch on the light to hear it properly, but,' he says, 'I think you've got a *splendid voice,* Charlie. A *splendid voice!*'"

We all agreed with that. Then Charlie says, "And then he says to me, 'But why do you do it almost at midnight, instead of at some other *reasonable* time, or in some *reasonable* place?'

"So I says to un," says Charlie, "Waal Vicar! I dun't generally draw up alongside the Vicarage until about that time! And I thinks to meself when I gets there, and I see the old Vicarage stuck up there and I knows you'm inside, — and I *knows* I don't go to Church very much, — I thinks to meself Well — 'tis good for you to know that there *is* religion and 'ymn-singen' and that *outside* the Church, as well as *inside!*'

"So the old Vicar 'e 'd say 'I appreciate that Charlie, I appreaciate that indeed! I know perfectly well,' he says, 'that there are a great many good people who never set foot in my Church except when they want to be baptised, or married, or buried. But,' he says, 'when we have *talent* and at the same time we have our religion in mind — I think we ought to *use* those talents we have!' And he says, 'The place to use a talent like that for singing hymns, isn't on the top of Vicarage hill in the middle of the night! The proper place — is in God's House!'

"'Well now,' he says, 'I'm trying to build-up the Choir to what it once was. And I put it to you, Charlie, that with a fine voice like yours, you could come and help me. You could put your talent to real use in the service of something you said you are already interested in — and that's your religion!'"

"Oh!" we said, and "Ah! Then 'e *'ave* ben an' asked thee to jine the Choir?"

"That's about the cut of it!" says Charl. "And do you know — I got two minds about it! What do you lot think I ought to do?"

So we give it a bit of thought. Then we says,

"Well, Charl you know — a voice like yourn — you ought to do as the Vicar says! 'Elp the old jugger out, — wun't to no no 'arm, — and' 'tis a good thing to sing well in the Church! We think you ought t' jine!"

And old Charl says, "I'm juggered if I don't!"

And o' course — that's how it all begun . . .

Well I 'ad my boy in the Choir at the time. I did get to Church fairly often — you cain't send your boy to Church and never go yourself can ye? But on that first Sunday marnen as old Charl turned-up for the Choir, you never seen such a turn-out in all your life . . .!

I should think there was as many folk there as come 'Arvest Festival or Christmas or Easter-time. All of us from the Wellington Arms look — all done up in our best — for to hear old Charl sing!

30

So up he went. Up the aisle, jes be'ind the Parson, solemn, wi' 'is cassock and 'is white shirt on, and my boy jes be'ind un. And they goes up into the Choir-place look, and Charl turns right, and the Vicar and my boy turns left, and there they was, a-facin' each other.

Well — Charlie didn't make much of a fist of the Responses 'cause he wasn't used to 'em like 'e is now. And 'e didn't know much about the Psalms. But when it come to *'ymn*-singin' that's when 'e opened up! And by gum — *didn't* 'e open-up . . .!

'Course, there's a big difference y' know, twixt singin' in the woods wi' nobody about, — to amuse yerself wi' the sound of your own voice bouncin' back off the trees, — and a-singin' inside our little old Saxon Church! Which is one of the *smallest* ones — so they d' say, — in the Country!

Anyways — old Charl give a gert cough — filled up 'is lungs — opened 'is mouth — and let drive! And that was the *end* o' singin' — for everybody else!

You never 'eard nothen like it! 'Twas a beller like old Farmer Vincent's bull!

My poor bwoy — 'e never *started* to sing! He jes stood there, starin' into old Charl's gert mouth — like 'e was turned to stone! Old Martha Myers on the argen as cain't play wi'out 'er book looked up frit to death — and that done it! She lost 'er place, — got all mixed up — and that didn't 'elp neither!

Them as did fancy theirselves singin' tried a few notes — but 'twas no good! Even that there Miss Gosney as sings 'igh in the Rumsedge Opera was beat in the end!

So nobody weren't singin — 'except old Charl and the Vicar! And you couldn't 'ear the Vicar, neither! All you could see was 'is jaw goin' up and down!

'Course we 'ad a darned good laugh about it up the Wellington and we says "Ah — *that* ain't gonna last!" But then, — as you know, — Charlie took Religion!

Yep — 'e took Religion! Took it up proper! 'E've never been in the Wellington from that day to this! He took on ringin' the bells, givin' the books out, lightin' the lamps — doin' the lot! 'E never missed nar sarvice!

Mind you — 'twas *useful!* It wanted *somebody* to 'elp out like that I s'pose — but that *voice* of his'n . . .!

Well that's why folk started droppin' off going to Church y' see. *Vicar's* all right — we all likes *he* — he don't preach a bad sermon, — but 'twas old Charlie's *racket!* Folk couldn't put up wi' it!

'Course — nobody said direct-like, why they 'ouldn't come! 'N I s'pose a man's got a right t' sing 'is 'eart out to 'is Maker if 'e feels so inclined! After all — the Vicar 'ad sart o' *converted* old Charlie! He'd a give-up the drink! He'd turned to the Church! 'E got 'isself wrapped up in it — so I s'pose it was like a sheep comin' back t' the vold! And the old Vicar always on about bein' the Shepherd of 'is little flock — 'e couldn't very well turn old Charlie out agen — could 'e?

I think he *did* drop a hint or two to old Charlie to tone it down a bit — but old Charl, once he d' get goin' — 'tis all or nothen — and that's it!

So there you are! We was stuck wi' it! And the old Vicar jest 'ad to put up wi' it! . . .!

31

Well — *I* was there the marnen old Charlie's voice — give out! 'Twas real comical . . .!

He'd a-gone through the Responses he'd a-learned by now, — jumpen in first like 'e used to and shoutin' ov 'em out so's nobody else 'ad a chance. He never *did* catch-on to the Psalms much. And then — we was movin' on up to the 'ymns!

Old Charl give 'is gert cough, drawed in 'is breath, opened-up 'is gert gravel-drain — and nar a sound come out!

'Course — we all *looked!* And there he was, huckin' about wi' 'is throat and rubbin' wi' 'is 'and but no — not nar sound . . .!

I cain't say as it wadn't a bit of a relief! Nobody sung for a minute or so — you know, used by now to leavin' it all to Charlie! But we started pickin' up yere and there, — and I yeard my bwoy singen' agen — first time for a twelvemonth — p'raps longer! And Miss Gosney stepped in and made herself heard jes like she used to — and we got on — and dang me we really *injied* ourselves — like we was a-singen for deliverance.

But — as you know — old Charlie's voice *'ad* gone! He went off down the Doctor's — as told 'im 'e'd got a parmenant weakness there! He'd a-tore a muscle in 'is throat, and 't'd healed together cock-eyed — or summat like that! — and he was never to raise 'is voice no more nor shout nor 'oller, else 't'd all 'appen agen!

And o' course — that was the end of old Charl — as a Choir-man!

Still — he never give up the Church as you know. He took-on the sexton's jobs and all that kind o' thing. He makes a beautiful job of trimming-up round the churchyard and sweepin' the paths — you can't deny! And folks as 'd gone over to Monkswell and down to Rumsedge started coming back agen. We got a fair congregation there now as nobody can't grumble over. And I *will* say although that there Miss Gosney does fancy 'erself a bit — she *do* sing well! And like I said to the Vicar, — jokin' — like — p'raps the Almighty *preferred* Miss Gosney to Charlie — and that's why 'E struck en dumb! But 'e never laughed . . .

But I *yeard* summat t'other day! And I'll tell thee what 'twas summat as takes a bit o' thinken' about . . .!

That nipper o' Charl's — I hadn't set eyes on him for — oh — best part of eighteen months I should think. Then I seed un in the village — and he *was* growed into a gert feller — no mistake!

I didn't get near enough to speak to un. But I met 'is Mother later on and I says I 'adn't seen young Garge for a long time and what a gert feller 'e'd a-got! I says,

"Where's he *ben* to?"

"Oh!" she says, "He went off to learn thatchin' on the other side o' Salisbury. Father didn't want him to be a hurdle-maker. 'Tis rough work — especially come the winter!"

"Well," I says. "Thatching ain't *easy* — is it?"

"No!" she says. "Well — 'e's home now. Father says if he really *wants* to be a hurdle-maker then he do — and that's that!"

I said "Well Missis — 'tis a good thing — Father and son workin' together! They ought to do well!"

"Oh — they do!" she says. And she says, "there's another thing about young George! You know his voice is broke?"

"No — *I* didn't know 'is voice was broke! But I s'pose 'tis about time! 'E's a big enough chap!"

"Yes!" she says' "I was up in the woods along wi' Charl the other day. 'Course you knows poor old Charl can't sing nor raise 'is voice no more! But while they was workin about — that boy started to sing!"

"Oh — did 'er?"

"Yes!" she says. "And do you know, he got a voice — well I thought *Charl* 'ad a *voice!* — but George's — he got one as'd knock poor Charlie's into a cocked hat! He got a *beautiful* vocie!" she says. "It did ring through that copse like a bell!"

I says "Oh! Sart of in'erited-like, then?"

"Yes!" she says. And she says, "Do you know what? He's going to join the Choir! 'E's going to take his Father's place — next Sunday!"

I looked at she you know! But d'you know what I zid as I stood there — in the mind? I zid my poor nipper, stuck up in the choir-stalls there, beat into silence *agean!* And a-starin' into another gate — big as old Charl's!

She says, "You know — the ways of the Lard *is* merciful! If He d' take away, — you can depend upon it He'll give back again — in His own good time!"

I says "Ah! And when He d' shut one gate Missis — hi'm juggered if He dun't awpen another!"

The Wheatear, one of our earliest summer visitors, arriving in March.
(Photograph: James Carr)

(I)
APRIL MORNING, 1947
The Countryside as it was.   Timsbury and Michelmersh.
(from the 1978 April issue of the Hants County Magazine)

They say — we have just been through the worst winter for sixty years. Grey, snowy skies. Stale, frozen snow on fields of concrete. A continuous grey haze, despite the bitterest winds I have ever known. And the seagulls losing strength as they come in every morning. Low over the ground, in loose formation. Crying piteously against a winter which starved them at the sea-shore, and yielded them nothing from the iron-faced land.

It went on for three months. And yet — look at April, now . . .

The beginning of the month saw the last of the snowdrops. But their life was short and sweet; they were delayed by the cold. And yet, while the blizzards came from the North, and the days were still short and dark, the long, straight, keeled, glaucous leaves thrust through the solid crust of earth. They pushed aside frozen carpets of leaf-fall, and crusts half of snow, half of ice, pressed down into the hollows. Then came the flower shoots. Then the blooms, still tightly closed, each on its slender, drooping stalk.

And there they hung. Waiting patiently for the sun which never came. Swinging in the bitter wind, whirling dry leaf-fall over them, and hissing through the laurel hedge behind.

Then after a while, they loosened — reluctantly. Just enough to show the green-tipped points of their white petals. And so they hung disconsolate, — until for a period of about two days we had sudden spells of weak sunshine.

And suddenly, they all opened in their chaste glory, as widely as they could. But now, Nature's clock had ticked on, and the hour was struck for their passing. It was a final, beautiful effort to live to the full at the very limit of their time — and then to pass away . . .

The tight, delicate, fleshy rosettes of primrose leaves had pushed through too; they had been sitting there, waiting, since January. There was a little sun at the beginning of the month. A few tiny members of the vanguard ventured forth where it was sheltered — but perished before the return of the cold spell.

Warned by this, no other blooms appeared. The leaf-rosettes busied themselves by becoming thick and fleshy. Tough, wrinkled, soft-haired leaves pushing aside and smothering the weed and the rubble, to make space for the coming blooms.

We watched, and waited. Buds eventually appeared at the rosette centres. They developed so far — then settled to wait for the better weather . . .

And at last it came. It was a poor showing of greenish-yellow sun-specs at first. Then — they all gathered strength together. And all down the bramble-banks, in the hollows, under the hazels, in the copse, on the laneside bank — there they are! Primroses . . . primroses everywhere . . .!

Even the daisy was delayed — until this month. Its green, tough, leathery rosettes like tiny cushions of spoons, were there on the lawn when the snow cleared. But by the beginning of April — still no flowers. The end of the cold spell still saw only tight-closed buds with crumpled white blouses peeping-

Opposite: In hollows, under hazels, in copse — there they are!
Primroses . . . primroses everywhere!   *(Photograph: Paul Carter)*

out from the calyx. But when the spring sunshine finally came, the daisy-patches opened quietly across the lawn — petals pink-tipped, eyes gleaming yellow as they are now . . .

Daffodils were late, too. The leaves hastened upwards from the ground in March — but no sign of flowers. Not until the second week in April did the dry spathes appear with the yellow gleaming through. And the orchard became awash with their nodding, cheerful, golden warmth — in place of the departed snowdrops.

So here they all are. All under the apple-trees, now beginning to bud. With the grass come to life around them, feeding on the leaf-fall. All along the feet of the ornamental firs and garden pines. All down the borders. And on through the village in every country garden, even down to the churchyard — a trail of yellow light. And the deeper gold of crocus, crowded round the aristocrat-crocuses, purple and mauve.

Since then — everybody's busy. Flaring dandelions — thick and regal in the rich earth of roadside banks — thin and starved on waste ground. White violets like fairy handkerchieves set on tiny springs. Their stouter blue and purple cousins, pushing aside trailers of old brown couch, to hitch their little chins round the brown blades so that the sun can look upon them.

The celandine spreads yellow pools in humid hollow and ditch, even in sheltered dips in the field. And already is vergeside grasses, under the hedges grown thick and smothered with pink hawthorn bud — the rich, burnished gleam of buttercup.

Only a few moments' sun, and the celandines will strain with all their might to open to the full. But there are still long hours of clouded skies. And then, the burnished-yellow carpet vanishes almost before your eyes as they all close. All you see then is the deep green of tangled, ground-hugging, heart-shaped leaves, and the yellow-green of closed petals.

Marsh marigolds, fleshy and matronly, glow in cushioned clumps the colour of richest butter, down in the old watermeadows.
Tantalisingly far enough into the riverside and swamp as to be unreachable. A good thing perhaps — because their blue-green, fleshy stems and roots are poisonous.

Wood-anemone runs dancing through copse undergrowth, and collects in gay crowds at the ride verge. The wood anemone is wind-shy; always turning her back towards it, her white bonnet sheltering her sweet, delicate fruits so that all you see is the bobbing head, the violet-and-blue markings on the backs of her petals.

The red deadnettle snatches what she can of April sunlight before the weeds grow up and shut her out. Sometimes she is with her sisters beside the gravelled path in dusty purple groups, and when the wind blows they scatter discarded blooms carelessly among the stones.

White stitchwort trails its delicate five-pointed cloven stars among tall grasses. Forget-me-nots show purple and crimson buttons in damp hollows. Broom and furze glow on the moor. Barren strawberry is in bloom; so, too, is mistletoe! And the cuckoo-pint leaves, splashed with tar, await the arrival of their hooded Lords and Ladies.

The leaves of the bluebell are already here. Clearing the way for next month's carpets of blue all through the copses, and beneath the woodland trees . . .

Opposite: The flaring dandelions of April before the great leaf of burdock.
(Photograph: Paul Carter)

36

(2)
APRIL MORNING, 1971
Michelmersh. The Countryside as it has become.

Let's go no further. It is the same on this side of the copse, as it was on the other. Only the green plants of barley show . . .

This is where the great grey-tyred monster with its green tank and long, steel antennae lumbered by, hissing its poison spray into the soil . . .

There are no spiders on the ground.

No ladybirds — to fly away home.

No little gauze-winged things.

Just soil, and the green barley . . .

This is where the footpath ran up from the Rosary. To Bellropes, and on up to the Church. In the old days, when there were children to come up from the Rosary, this is the way they came . . .

But that was before the copse fell into destruction, and decay. Trees raced each other for light — the winners strangled the losers. So they stand; strange, tall tree-corpses, with the home of the woodpecker in their heads. Branches strewn across fences; a kind of tree graveyard — all dead.

Here is a curious metal structure, read and eaten into holes with rust.

What is it?

Does anybody know?

Is it the ruin and the wreck of a charcoal-kiln?

Does anybody in the village remember a charcoal-burner up at Park? Is there anybody *left* to remember?

No — no-one remembers . . .

Only the beeches live; tall, with a green mass of downward-sweeping, smooth-skinned branches, the sunlight quite still upon them. Green tips of leaves bursting from spindle sheathes.

Does anyone remember the Carpenter, with his wooden lathe, who made furniture from beechwood and sold it in the village? Is there any of it left?

Does anyone know where he had his shop?

No — no-one knows . . .

This is where Farmer John lived. This was his apple-tree. This was his orchard. This wild tangle was the hedge which his wife trimmed so neatly, with so much loving care.

This was his garden — and these few stones are where his house stood.

Then the big man came, and pulled the house down. But he kept the sheds, and the barns, and the yards. Strange that such buildings, to house farm implements, are now more important than dwellings for human beings, — looking for somewhere to live . . .

Yes — on this side, it's just the same. A great expanse of featureless green . . .

Look — the roots of the old hedge which used to shelter the footpath. Down there, a lonely, forlorn style, marking the site where it used to be . . .

Here's one hedge still left. Ralph Wightman — does anyone remember him now? — the Wessex countryman who spoke for Britain in the darkest days of the War — he must have seen it laid, pleached and solid in the days when he came this way to visit the Curtisses, who farmed Park long before Farmer John.

But it is now neglected, outgrown; with great holes you could drive a tractor and trailer through. It cannot be long before it, too, will be rooted out. And the green prairie will become larger and more featureless than before.

Down there — a modern milking parlour. An angled, utilitarian thing — it does not pretend to be beautiful. It sits uneasily, even in this featureless land.

And up on the hill, beyond the trees, what we are pleased to call these days a 'Dutch barn'. Just a double row of upright girders, with sharp, hard angles for a roof.

Why, seeing that you and I cannot put-up a garden shed without planning permission, in case it spoils the countryside, are such things allowed to be there?

It wasn't always so. Farm buildings still linger of a bygone age. Beautiful. Complementing the countryside — not intruding upon it. But relics of an age that is no more . . .

The edge of the village. A lovely old cottage — standing empty. Waiting for a buyer at a price which you and I, and no young country couple who might want to stay in the village where they were born, to bring up their country children, can afford. Who will just as likely buy it, stay a while to renovate it, then offer it for an even more fantastic price — and pass on his way . . .

I see the hoeing-gangs, singling and singing across the hill. I see the great black Shires with bobbing heads, chains jingling, fringes trembling at fetlock as they step with incredible daintiness along the furrow.

I hear the old cries, "Whoa!" — "Hook-off!" — "Hut-hut!" — "Whey-up!" The ploughman's rough, clear voice — "Get up there, Di'min! Get on — will 'e?"

And up among the beeches of old Park Farm, the cry at six o'clock in the morning and about three in the afternoon, "Come on en! Cup — cup — come on 'en! Cup-cup-cummalong!"

And across the Downs there, the milking-herd, hearing it, lumbering leisurely to its feet. And sailing like a white-and-brown convoy towards the voice, until it vanishes behind the trees . . .

They've left this piece. It belongs to the cottage on the other side of the footpath. The dandelions flare. The white deadnettle is out. There's a magnificent cuckoo-pint, down there in the damp shadows . . .

The daisies are out on the lawn. The periwinkle blooms in the shade of the thatch . . .

The Scots Pine still towers in its corner, its skin kissed by the sun . . .

Beware Woolly Aphis!

Thirty — perhaps forty years ago . . .

The family Pride and Joy was the Wireless Set. A handsome piece. In a wooden cabinet, with an open-fretwork design of sunset, — or was it sunrise? __ covering the loud-speaker. And from out of that speaker came crackling the terrible warning — "Beware — Woolly Aphis!"

It seemed that this monster was about to be let loose in our orchards and gardens, with evil intent. I was clattering away on my old, cast-iron-based Oliver typewriter, its type set on steel hoops, as the dire message came through. I wondered how the monster would creep-up on us. At night — through the neighbouring copse? Or was it already lurking and watching, a shapeless, woolly form, behind the garden hedge?

Perhaps I'd better stop and listen . . .

The voice went on —

"Woolly Aphis is a serious pest to your apple-trees! It surrounds itself with a mass of wool-like threads, and it's the *wool* that makes it so difficult to control. So as soon as you see these tufts, get a stiff brush, dip it in methylated spirits and get them off!"

It was, of course, Mr Middleton, the Radio Gardener. Did you ever get his All-the-Year-Round Gardening Guide? I did. I still use it now. If it's only to tell me, — when I consult it, — that what I'm going to do in the garden is already three weeks or a month too late!

"Look to the Spring and Winter greens!" he writes.

What Spring and Winter greens? Those miserable little plants which stopped dead in winter at six inches high, until the final rot-off at the stem in January? Or those gelatinous green lumps which finally emerged from the last fall of snow?

"Plant-out sprouts!" he writes.

All right — I'll *plant* them! And so will my rival up the road . . .

I know what will happen to *his*. Five feet high with leaves a foot across by September. And Brussels sprouts for Christmas, and right on up to the middle of February next year. And if he spots me he'll hold up a button between finger and thumb and he'll say,

"'Ow's *that* for a sprout then? 'Ard as iron and bigger 'n a golf-ball!"

And I know what will happen to *mine*! About ten inches high, some three feet — the odd four-footer if I'm lucky! I *might* see some decent buttons on the four-footer! Not quite as big as golf-balls — but big enough. And to my dear wife I shall say,

"Perhaps this year we shan't do so badly!"

And she'll say,

"Pick them *now*! We've got a *freezer*! Do you understand that? Do you know what I *mean*? A *freezer*!"

And I'll say,

"I think we'll hang-on a bit, and let them get bigger!"

And they will! And then all of a sudden, when I'm not looking, they'll fluff-out and become *useless* for freezing — and not much good for cooking either! And just before Christmas my wife will be bringing back Brussels sprouts from Romsey with her shopping, and she'll throw them on the kitchen table without a word!

And *I* shan't say a word — either . . .!

MAY MORNING 1976
The Hampshire Test, from source to mouth.

We ask at Overton for the bridge. The first one below the source of the Test . . .

Not everyone seems to know. Not even in Overton . . .

The Test is *supposed* to rise near Ashe, on this Overton side of Whitchurch. But a local bailiff tells me the Ashe spring has not been active for some time. And that the Test only *really* gets going on a farm about three quarters of a mile down from Ashe.

Anyway, here's the bridge. We turn right a little beyond it, and carry-on until we come to the end of the road. We'll leave the car. I'll get permission at the farm house . . .

It's down here — down the footpath to the right. We shall see it when we come to the footbridge . . .

There it is — over on the left. That twig-filled pool under the bush. That's it — the unlikely, but in fact true beginning of one of the most famous trout-fishing rivers in the world. A slow, finger-depth trickle, bramble-bordered, coming from the pool and under the bridge, carrying with it little blackened fragments of humus. But even here, since there are only three of us, quiet and easy-moving, it's a beautiful beginning . . .

Those thin, straight, brilliantly-coloured twigs on rustling wings, crossing and recrossing the space between brook and bridge, are damsel-flies. All shades of green and blue; some dark, some brilliant.

There's one at rest. Green body, green-tinted transparent wings held vertically. And red eyes.

A quite audible clatter near our faces! It's the dragon-fly; much more robust and multi-coloured, pincer-tailed, as he swoops by. Purple hindwings, and white fore-wings.

There's a movement, — only slight, — on the end of that twig. It's another dragon-fly. Yellow-brown and black, stump-bodied; transparent yellow and black-spotted wings, held flat and stiff, according to his tribe.

He stares from his perch with dark-brown eyes, to swoop upon the unwary like a bird of prey. He sallies. He's on that other twig above the water on the other side.

He sallies again. He's back to his original post. So that's his beat, where he snatches his victims. They could be other insects, or one of his own kind. When he catches them he'll tear them to fragments and eat them, piece by piece, while they're still alive.

Back down the footpath — and look down the vale! Dozens of springs here. Making a sort of elongated little lake with sedge and reed all round the sides.

Plenty of activity down near the Kingcups. Fleshy green-leaved, and blooms like goblets brimmed to overflowing with sun-melted butter. Poisonous, of course.

House-martins, stepping delicately. Balancing themselves with upraised steel-blue wings and tail, keeping their white vests clear of the mud for which they shovel.

Do you know how they carry it? Watch . . .

They lodge it above their beaks, against their foreheads. Then when they get to the eaves of the cottages up high there on the bank, they press it to make yet another layer upon the inverted dome-shaped structures of their

41

nests. With luck, they'll finish them before the sparrows come trying to take them over. By then, they'll leave an entrance-hole too small for the sparrows to get in.

There are swallows there, too. With their green-glossed backs, long wings and tail streamers. And their chestnut foreheads and throats and blue cravats and pale buff waistcoats.

But they are birds of flight — clumsy on the ground. They land only briefly — and then set-off to the garage or the barn, where the nest sits like a saucer on a rafter close to the roof, with just enough space for the hen to slip sideways in and out, which she does because of her elongated wings and tail.

Not all of them are nest-building. Some — can you hear them whispering as they come? — flash across marigold and yellow water-lily, pickin-off insects as they go. Some go up with the swifts, scimitar-winged, screaming with the excitement of it all — who says wild creatures don't enjoy a bit of fun? See? The swallows in front now — the swifts close behind, skimming the barn-tops! Now the swifts ahead — but slowing down so that the swallows can catch-up again!

"I do know Willie! I *do* know Willie! I DO know Willie — yes!" That's the pigeon! He'll keep telling us this all the time we're here — from inside the sunlit heads of those tree-tops. The soft voices of warblers everywhere — and there's the cuckoo, just above ourheads! When he 'cuckoos' and you're so close — it doesn't sound a clear call at all, does it? It sounds as if he's got a touch of the bronchitis!

When we go back — we'll pause on the bridge and look over. Then we'll see the headwaters of the Test truly rippling on their way . . .

We'll go now through Whitchurch, down to Hurstbourne Priors, and on down to Longparish . . .

Longparish is anglers' land. The river is completely changed. It moves - determinedly. With a great weight of water which those who maintain hatch, bank and bridge, learn to respect.

Alternating shallows and deeps, and lush growth on the banks of that coarse, grass-like, solid-stemmed plant called 'sedge'. It grows lush like that because Harold Dobson, the water-keeper here, burns it off in March. He says the angler likes it, — if it's controlled properly. It conceals the angler from the fish. But he gets a bit annoyed if it grows tall enough to interfere with his casting.

It's weed-troubled country. Those long fronds in the water are pondweed. It's a brittle plant — and has to be strictly controlled. Even the smallest piece to break off will grow again.

The one near to it is starwort. It's called that because of the shape of its head rosette of leaves. It rises up now, from the warm bottom currents where it spends the winter.

Those platforms of floating leaves with crowds of white, five-petalled, yellow-eyed simple flowers growing out of them, are crowfoot. Some have curved their stalks down to ripen the fruit below the water — they do that when they've been fertilised. And if you look in these little, still bays, you'll see the lilac flowers of water-violet with its ferny leaves below the surface.

Harold told me the weeds are cut at set times that everybody knows who

Opposite: The Test at Longstock.   *(Photograph: Gerd Franklin)*

live on the banks of the river — otherwise there would be chaos. But it's a very skilled job. Cut too high — you collect silt, and lay a bed for more weed. Too low — and all the trout you've stocked on your stretch will move-off to somebody else's, because you've got to have *enough* weed-life for them to find food.

That's odd — hurdles set in the middle of the river! If you look, you'll see they're set to deflect the current, and that controls silt. There will be purple loosestrife and giant willow-herb on the banks towards the end of the month — at least, it should be just beginning to show.

Be careful about collecting riverside flowers. Especially those which look like parsley or celery gone to seed; some of them are very poisonous.

We'll go on now through Forton and on to Wherwell, ('Wurrel' as the country locals say,) and we'll call in at the Seven Stars, which is on the bank of the river near Chilbolton . . .

You see — it's all changed again. The river is wide, and faster flowing. There's mother mallard steering her brown breast into the current, quacking at her thistledown sprinkling of ducklings so light they seem to be frantically treading on top of it. They look as if at any moment they'll be swept away . . .

We can walk from the pub garden to the point where the Anton comes in from Andover.

Can you hear that triple whistle? Like someone playing a flute! Up beyond those yellow flags, look. There's two slim brown birds with long bills, bowing to each other as if they were hinged on their long, red shanks! Just beyond them, there's a rather darker brown-backed one, on even longer *green* legs!

It's only a small tributary — the Anton — but where it joins the Test is the beginning of the middle 'slowing-down' stage of the river. To see that properly, we'll go on down to Mottisfont . . .

Over the Railway Bridge — the old Redbridge-Andover Sprat and Winkle line, it isn't there any more, — turn right and take the road past Stockbridge to Romsey. Through King's Somborne with all its thatch and its lovely old Church. Over and round the edge of the Downs. Round the Rosary and past the chalk-pits on our left, started originally to build the Southampton-Andover canal. A bit further down now — and there's the sign-post, pointing to Mottisfont.

There's the Station houses on your right, with one old servant of the Southern Railway, Jim White, still living in one of them. One of the finest gardeners I know.

And there's the Station — or was; it's a private house now. Standing by the de-metalled remains of the same Sprat and Winkle line. The platforms are still there. The goods yards were over there, where Jim runs his goats. My Grandfather was Station-master here in the 1920's. There was his wife, seven daughters, (one died in infancy,) and a son all packed in that little Station house at one time — I don't know how they all fitted in! Kate was the one who died. Only two left now; my Mother Ida, and Aunt Nora who lives a couple of fields away from me in the next village, Timsbury. They must have memories . . .

We'll stop off the road, just beyond the bridge . . .

Look upriver. Long, lazy sweeps of a much wider and deeper stream, meandering its way in giant curves through the farm land of the valley

*Longparish is weed-fronted country, both in the river and on the banks.
Harold Dobson (now retired) tackling the problem.*

floor. Farm houses on distant hills. Trees on the horizon, heat-hazed to a faint, distant blue . . .

Heifers — they've got the fly! There they go, tails aloft like flags, one behind the other, jumping the dyke . . .
Silage-time. There's a man across there look, sat down between the windrows, snack on the ground between his legs, bottle to his lips — I wonder what he's got in it?

Martins, brown-and-white this time — sandmartins — there they go up and down and back and forth behind the harvester, gape open for the insects the harvester disturbs. Some quartering the river for gnats and other flies that hatch in the water. One coming in under the bridge look — against the breeze. See how it tacks its wings like sails to get through? *There* it goes — scudding away over the tall netting round Jim's chicken-run in the old Station yard . . .

You can see how the silt comes down — the water's clear — but brown. There's a great weight of water down there — piling against the stanchions, before it saunters on down to the sea . . .

Look — there's a little silver torpedo set-out from the bank! It's a water-shrew — silver like that because of the air-bubbles trapped in its fur. A bit of a foolhardy journey — I don't think it will beat the current across to the other side! No — it isn't going to — it's being swept down towards us. Tiny legs going like mad, wee tail desperately ruddering!

Get back a bit — and keep still! Down there look — that shape, refraction-broadened, sliding out from the shadows! Olive-brown back, black and grey-blue-ringed spotted, hooked old jaw! It's the wily old King trout nobody can catch! See — he rolls up a honey-gold, dark-pupilled eye — brakes on his fins, and with one lazy old sweep of his tail he slides back into cover again.

I wonder if he was after that poor little shrew — or was it too big for him? Anyway the *shrew* thinks so — it's on the surface, panicking — lost its way. There it goes, carried under the bridge — to a fate unknown!

Plop! — what was that? Over there look — that ring of ripples just under those shredded stalks on the bank! Can't see anything. Only the ripples widening and also passing under the bridge. I don't know though — *there's* another shape under the water — just going in under that overhang! I reckon it was a water-vole.

Time to move on . . .

We're coming up to Timsbury Bridge. Ugh! See that insect stuck on the windscreen with a burst abdomen? Black,— with lacy transparent wings and three long hairs — over an inch long — attached to its tail. Look at them — they're exploding all over it — we're into a swarm of them. Better slow down and use the wipers! See how they seem to hover upright just before we smash into them? They're Mayflies. I expect we shall hit another swarm when we go over Greatbridge.

A field-day for the trout! Some of these Mayflies emerge from nymph to the winged state on the surface of the water. If we stopped to watch, we'd see minute whirlpools directed to and engulfing one floating dun after another — the trout sucking them in below. In some years, even the streets of Romsey have been filled with these swarms. They're males. Like the bees, they move-off after the females when they appear, and the mating takes place high up and in mid-air.

Through Romsey — Hampshire's 'Little Venice' as it's called on account of the streams around it and running below its streets. Up Pauncefoot Hill to Totton. Turn right at the traffic-lights, over the railway crossing to Eling Wharf. We'll leave the car at the Anchor. We'll go up over the bridge to the Church and take the footpath down through the Churchyard to Goatee Beach.

And there's the end of the story . . .

The long edge of the port of Southampton lies along the distant opposite bank of the river, with all its innumerable details. Odd ends of streets run down to riverside roads peeping through trees. Steeples, like upthrust, pointing fingers. One dominant — but now insignificant beside pylons and the dehumanising gigantism of modern blocks and towers. Low hills crowded by the port's houses . . .

Then comes the grey, motley mass of masts, funnels, cranes, dockside structures, stretching away to the right in a sweeping curve miles long until they all seem jumbled together on the skyline like a bundle of pins.

We'll go on down towards the fields. See how tide-ravage has carved deep, smooth U-channels into what, not so long ago, were green fields. Now they're split-up more and more into isolated islands with thatching reed growing on the top, higher than a man. With inch-wide, foot-long leaves all up the stem, and purplish-brown plumes here and there already becoming grey with silky hairs.

Endless small-bird chatter inside them. And there's a brown reed-warbler sliding up one of the stems into view to the very top of the reed, to sing his tuneless little song.

Listen! From over the docks, the crowded outlines, and across the wide gleam of the river-mouth, comes wavering the sound of the Civic Centre clock, striking the hour. Two o' clock! We'll just get back to the Anchor in time for a quick one . . .!

"The re-assuring long thatched roof of our cottage" — Mrs. West further figure, with "foster-brother" Leonard beside her. Foreground, Mrs. Schammel, wife of sailor Schammel (see p. 7).

VERNON

When I was very small, my foster-Father used to take me up in the Churchyard, to watch him cut the grass. And when I became a nuisance, he would tell me to go away and play. And he'd say,

"Dun't thee jump on the mounds, boy! And dun't get into no mischief!"

I remember wandering along the pathway and passing below rows of diamond-leaded windows in the South wall. On under the ancient yew by the porchway, and on again round the West end of the Church. And standing there, uncertain. For down in a damp hollow, stood a long, low shed, with a padlocked door . . .

I had once seen Father open it, and push out a long yellow shape on tall wire wheels, into the sunlight. I watched him set the handles of this curious trolley — click click! Click click! I watched him oil the wheels.

I asked him what it was for. But he said, "Never you mind, boy!" But I found out. The very next day, I was in the front garden. I heard peoples' boots crunching on the gravelled road. I peered through the hedge.

There was Father, coming straight towards me, with a tall black hat on and a black coat with tails, and black boots and trousers. He looked very grave. The yellow trolley was being pushed along behind him, and on it was a long narrow box, covered in flowers. Then followed lots of grave-faced men and women. And some of them were crying . . .

The spectacle sent me rigid with fear. It looked as if they would all come straight through the hedge, into the garden. But at the last minute they all turned to go up Church path. Their boots tramped-tramped on the other side of the hedge before me, and the womens' black skirts swished as they went along.

I knew, therefore, that the trolley had something to do with this dreadful affair. Rather than go by the shed in which it was housed, I decided to turn back. But at that moment, I saw Vernon.

He was a little beyond the shed, standing between two graves. Fingers of one hand on his mouth, he stood looking at me. He was very curiously dressed. He wore a bright red dress, covered by a white pinafore. Tilted to the back of his head, was a straw hat with an enormous brim.

We stood and looked at each other for a long time. Then he said,

"Are you coming out to play?"

So I plucked up enough courage to run past the shed with the horrid thing in it. And we played 'houses' — laying out a grass 'house' with the trimmings of the day before.

The game went on for a long time. I suppose it was during the course of it that I heard the little boy's name.

Then I became aware that Father was watching. He said, "Who be you talkin' to then, boy?"

"I'm talking to Vernon!"

"Vernon? Who'se 'Vernon'? *I* cain't see no Vernon!"

I looked round. "He's gone in," I said.

Father laughed.

"Oh ah! Well — you'd better come on down along wi' me! 'Tis dinner time!"

After this, foster-Father did not go up to the Churchyard for a very long time. His real job was a thatcher; he did sexton and verger to make a little more money.

I often thought of Vernon. I asked Father when we would be able to go

49

again. But he said he was too busy "elsewheres".

In the end, I decided to go myself . . .

I was playing on the lawn, under the greengage tree, when I made my decision. The garden gate was partly open. I hesitated. Then I looked carefully around to make sure I was not seen — and slipped through.

Greatly excited I ran along the footpath beside the road, and through Church Path gate. About half-way up the hill, I came to the great oak beside the school playground. I stopped to look back.

The reassuring, long thatched roof of the cottage showed above the willows. The bedroom windows were open. The white curtains hung motionless in the sun.

Anyway I ran again; up between the great, straggling briar-hills. I came to the tall hollybank; turned — and there was the silent Churchyard.

Rows of headstones stared, with blank grey faces. As if they had suddenly stopped talking, because I had no business to be there.

I was uneasy — but I went on. The rattle of a pebble at my foot startled me. In the sunlit heads of the cypresses, I heard the soft and familiar "Croo-croo, Croo-croo!" of pigeons.

A lark swept up past the steeple. It poised its quivering cross above me, and began to fill the silence with its song.

I felt a little better. I went on beneath the tall rows of windows in the south wall. I looked up at the curious formal pictures, out-lined in lead. All white and lifeless from where I stood — quite different from the wonderful reds and purples and golds they contained inside the Church.

Then I had to pass the porch doors. These too, stared. With gigantic, blank, pointed faces. And behind them, I could hear the whispering echo of my own light footfalls.

The pigeons stopped "crooing". The thrush flew away. The lark drifted down out of sight. All was silent again . . .

Suddenly, I had an awful thought! I knew this was God's House.

And God — might be *inside* — listening! And I knew that God was a giant — else why should the doors of His house be so tall?

I raced on, and turned the corner, out of His sight. But I was faced then with the horrid little house with the *thing* in it on wire wheels! Where were all those sad people dressed in black? Were they all inside that house too?

Oh how I wished I had not come! I could not go back past the porch doors, in case God had opened them and was waiting there, tall above the tall steps! I could not go back through the grey-faced throng of headstones. Nor again venture under the dark yew-tree's frown.

Then, I heard a noise like a footfall on the pebbled path! I fairly flew past the horrid little house — round the next corner — and Vernon was there! He was there, swinging on the Vicarage garden gate. I shouted "Run-run! *God's* coming!" — and we both fled down through the Vicarage gardens.

I followed him — under the walnut trees; up along a pathway leading to straggled rhodedendrons and tall birches on the other side of the Vicarage grounds. He vanished among them; and when I caught up with him, he was struggling with an old, rusted gate. I helped him, and we just managed to squeeze through.

We were through — we were in *Vernon's* place — we were safe! We sat down on the grass together, and laughed and laughed! We stopped, looked at each other, and laughed again.

When we had quietened down, I looked round. We were at the back of a long squat cottage. I could not see the roof; it was too high. I cannot recall all that we did, but I do retain a few clear images.

At the corner of the house by a drainpipe, was an enormous stone. We tugged it over, to see the 'grandfathers' underneath. They rolled themselves into bullet-like balls. We picked them up and gently squeezed them, to see them half open and to see their rows of legs and waving antennae.

There was a great wooden water-butt in a corner between the back porch and the ivied scullery wall. We could just climb high enough to see the sky, the clouds, the side of the house, and our two faces reflected in the still water. We saw kicking, shooting 'squigglers'; which kicked themselves off into the depths when we reached down to touch them, then came sailing leisurely to the surface again.

I looked in at the back porch. The house had no door on it — only two bent and rusted hinges. The inside was black, and stained. An acrid, stale smell came from out of it. I remember thinking I would not like to live in there!

It was time to go. I said to Vernon,

"I don't want to go back through the Churchyard!"
He said, "You can go the other way. I'll show you!"

So I followed him along another path, which led all along the bottom of the Vicarage grounds. We came out into the road just above Taylor's pond. I knew where I was then. I hurried on down the hill. I heard Vernon calling "Goodbye . . .! Goodbye . . .!"

I turned to wave. I could not see him, nor the gate he had come from. I could not see a path, or a house — just nothing but the Vicarage hedge, and the school playground which lay below it. But I could still hear his voice — "Goodbye . . .! Goodbye . . .! It seemed to float upwards into the tree-tops. And it changed. "Cuckoo! Cuckoo! Cuk-Cuk-Cuk-Cuckoo . . .!

I ran on . . .

Foster-Mother had been hunting the garden. Father stood, puzzled, in the ivied porch, looking across the lawn. The scroop of the gate as I opened it made him look sharply and say,

"It's all right! He's back! Where you *been* boy!"

"I been playing with Vernon."

"But you came out of the school playground," said Mother. "You must have come down the *road!* I been *watching* Church Path!"

I said "That's where Vernon's house is! You goes through the Churchyard and down in the Vicarage garden and the down in the trees and through a gate as won't open proper, — and you comes to Vernon's!"

Father suddenly stopped smiling. I was pleased I could tell them something they did not know. I told them all about Vernon's house; the big stone with the grandfathers under it, the water-butt and the squigglers. The inside — black, and stained, and smelly.

Father asked what Vernon looked like. I told him about his red dress, his overall, and the big sun-hat he wore.

There was a long silence. Suddenly, I saw Mother's face was all white, and strange. It frightened me. I burst into tears — but I could hear their voices through my own cries.

I heard Mother say "Well he *couldn't* have done!"

Then I was swept up into foster-Mother's arms and she was concerned with comforting me. "It's all *right* boy — you 'aven't done anything *wrong* — you 'aven't *done* anything wrong!"

But it was all a great puzzle. I *knew* I hadn't done anything wrong. So why did they keep saying I must never go up to the Churchyard nor down past the Vicarage on my own again . . .?

Well — it was all a long time ago. My foster-Mother has been dead these forty years past. Foster-Father outlived her by a decade or so.

I used to visit them quite often through the years. I carried on visiting Father, up to the end . . .

Kent's buses were running in those days. The driver always recognised me. He'd stop outside the cottage without me asking. I'd get up from my seat, say 'Cheerio', and walk across the green. And through all the years, the gate that Mr Atkins the blacksmith had made up at the forge, would always give its same familiar 'scroop' as I pushed it open.

The last time I saw Father on his feet, he had become an old man. His son Leonard lived with him and his daughter-in-law, Gertie. They all pressed me to stay the night . . .

In the evening, we talked of old times. Of boys I had once played with at Baughurst, who had become middle-aged, like myself. With families, and respectable rural businesses.

I said to Father, "Then there was *Vernon.* What happened to him?"
He tried to recollect.

"Vernon . . .? Vernon . . .? Oh ah — the little boy you played wi' in the churchyard! Oh — we never saw no more of 'im! Never seen no more of 'im from that day to this!"

I was a bit perplexed. I said.
"What do you *mean,* Father?"

Father looked perplexed, too. Then he said,
"Well — 'e never turned up no more!"

"Never turned up?" "No!"

He looked at me — strangely. He said,

"But you *knows* about Vernon, — don't ye?"

"Know? How *could* I know? I haven't seen sight nor heard sound of him since my own people came and took me to live with them!"

"No!" he said. "I s'pose you ain't! I s'pose you was took away afore it could all be explained to 'e!" And he went on —

"There never *was* no Vernon boy, — not in *your* time! There was when *I* was a boy! And there was a cottage — where you said. *And* a path to it from the churchyard as you went down.

"But that cottage took fire — long years ago! The Mother and Father got out — but the little boy didn't! They both thought t'other 'd brought 'im out wi' em — but when they found 'e was still in there they both runned back to get 'im! And then it all fell in and they were all burned! They was all burned to death!"

I looked at foster-Father, and he looked at me.

"I *can't* believe it!"

"'Tis true! True as you and me sett'n yere talkin' about it!"

"Well!" I said. "How do you *account* for it, Father? How do you account for me *seeing* the boy and playing with him and talking to him? And the house — and the water-butt — all those things?"

I could see Father didn't know what to say. He puffed at his pipe. Then he took it from his mouth, fingered-down the baccy and said,

"We never *'ave* accounted for it, boy! Nobody ain't never been able to 'count for it all!"

(I)
JUNE MORNING 1972, "Sunshine".
Goatee Beach, Eling. Along the shoreline towards Marshwood.
Into the woods and on out the other side.

Up through the woods we go. Lazy shades of summer, scattered on leaf-mould paths . . .

We pass through an almost tropical abundance of June flowers. Red campion, ragged robin. St John's wort, bright yellow; the purple mallow, the dusty-bloomed bramble. Enchanter's nightshade with its branches of tiny pink flowers, and cysts in the stalks of its leaves, pellucid against the light. Ranks and companies of rosebay willowherb assembling at the coppice edge, preparing for their rosy-purple display in a week or a fortnight's time. Barley beyond them, bowed in submission as it awaits the seed-merchant's traveller with his measuring-stick and board, to see if the grain is suitable for the brewers.

A great, hot, sticky silence. Bird song desultory. Territories are now settled. There is no longer need to be at one's post at dawn guarding one's patch, challenging all comers. The business of setting-up house is over, save for a few late warblers; rearing the family will soon be over. Also it will soon be moulting-time, and that's uncomfortable. One doesn't feel like singing . . .

Dry mould underfoot becomes sandier. We pass through birch-groves; on into pines where the air, damp and sickening-sweet, oppresses; — the trees themselves seem to drain us of energy. We tread sour carpets of last year's needles.

Cobweb strands here and there — cling to our perspiring faces. Where the lumbermen cleared last year, there stands a forest of bracken as high as our shoulders.

A large red-and-black-and-white butterfly sits silhouetted on a low cluster of gleaming pine needles. So still. So perfectly outlined against blue sky, it looks like a collector's specimen, artifically mounted. You can see its slender antennae, its legs bent at the knee. I think it's a Red Admiral.

It's off — fluttering. But you know — butterflies don't *really* flutter. If you look carefully at that weak and floppy-looking motion, you'll see that it's as strong and purposeful and controlled as a bird's.

There's a Peacock — and a Blue . . . And small Browns there, on the brambles . . .

We're through now. Heath and heather in long, purple smudges across the moor. The track, sandy; leading-on between red-purple mats to the long, low, distant crest crowned by more pines, and beyond them, banks of oak and beech grey-green in the hillside haze . . .

No relief — from the heat. The moor and the scene beyond, shimmers, and wavers . . . Let's get under that pine-tree and sit on a log.

Keep still! Keep stock-still! Something — I saw it out of the corner of my eye — in that little patch of sand — moved like lightning! Keep still . . . watch . . .!

There look! There it comes — that tiny movement in the top of that clump of heather. It's the same colour as the clump, but concentrate your eyes! See it? See its little fingers clinging on? A wee lizard — the furze-evat.

There's another on the sand — and another — and another! Side-by side! Chests off the ground, bent arms, 'pigeon-toed' if you can say that about fingers and hands. As if they're doing press-ups — but their heads turned to one side — and all utterly still!

A Forester told me that if you whistle, quietly, they might stay long enough to clap your hand and catch one! If you're not quick enough he said, you might catch only its tail — and it'll run off leaving its tail broken-under your fingers!

Let's try!

Gone! Even the one in the furze!

So much for *that* story!

They say the furze-evat *bears* its young. I don't know if that's true or not. The sand-lizard doesn't — it lays eggs and covers them with a thin sand-layer to hatch-out in the sun.

I know *that's* true, because I've found them — like wee parchment-dabs. And wondered at their toughness when I tried to pull them apart.

There's a whinchat over there — on top of that thistle-head. That little yellow-brown bird that keeps fanning its tail . . .! It's decided we're harmless! It's giving us a quivery little song . . .!

(2)
JUNE MORNING 1972, "Showers."
Carsbrook Common

It isn't a thunder-shower. There's no thunder about . . .

Let's wait awhile under that horsechestnut tree . . .

That's Sid Head's cottage. That thatched one up there, built of planks. They say he built it himself. I wonder why they painted it red?

They get their water from the spring there — down by the road. It's a long path to trudge up — with buckets of water . . .

It's stopped now. Shall we move-on? Hang on a minute — listen . . .!

Step out here. *There* it is — right on the highest pinnacle in the copse — the storm-thrush! *There* — you can see its white breast, — you can even see the black spots on it! — facing the sun!

Everything gleaming wet; the trees, the hazels. The copse floor warm, and damp, like a sponge. And besides the drips, you can hear myriad beads of moisture seeping into the leaf-mould; a soft, singing noise pervading the whole copse.

Life stirs in the soil. Beetles and other crawling things come out from under the leaves and stones where they have sheltered. They move in the moss, rustle in the leaf-mould.

Opposite: "Up through the woods we go. The lazy shades of summer, scattered on leaf-moulded paths . . ." (A Robin Fletcher picture of Dame's Slough in the New Forest)

You can smell damp, sweet, pure earth. Or is it so pure . . .? All the stench from chemicals sprayed on the fields; from diesel lorries in lanes, from tractors and motor-cars has been washed down into it. Where it goes from there — who knows?

The storm-thrush has left his pinnacle. He has left the trees below him, the wet tangle, the leaves beaten to the ground, the secret insect-hosts beneath them. Now he's become quiet, you can hear softer voices. The long trill of warblers. The robin — making a few inconsequential comments. The distant nightingale. All as fascinating in their way as the storm-cock — again busy spellbinding from another pinnacle, but now faint and far away.

And startling, repellant, a huge insult in the broad, bucholic voice of some ignorant rook! Shouting his obsenities in his rough country speech — a bony, ragged, giant of a fellow — no manners, no finesse. No grace, no song to spread like gossamer down through the valley on a wet summer's day. He can be loved for nothing like that!

He comes out after the rain to shovel in the mud for grubs and other disgusting things — too coarse and large for the dainty appetites of the song birds.

And yet — he isn't a bad old fellow! He's *very* intelligent! The countryside would seem empty without him . . .

The drips increase — the wind stirs. There's a radio going on and on inside Sid Head's cottage, and voices, muffled by its walls. There's a spider there — it looks transparent, — dropping a strand from one rail in the fence to another . . .

Time to move on. Or we'll be late for lunch . . .

The Shelley Mob

Old Man Bungey was the Senior Citizen of the Shelley Mob. We were the fairly small group of lads and lasses who worked on the Shelley Nurseries at the back of the Vyne, at Ower, in 1946.

The face the old man turned to the world was unsmiling, but not unfriendly. It was long, lined, expressionless. But there was often a twinkle in his pale blue eyes.

He was an old-time countryman. Cloth-capped, open-necked shirted, a broad leather belt with a big brass buckle; sometimes coduroys, and boots generally, whereas we all wore Wellies.

I don't think he was an agnostic. I've never yet met a true country-man who doesn't believe in *something*. But he had two hates. The Gentry. And Churches.

One day, Harry Glasspool the Foreman picked out five of us; Old Man Bungey, his son Bob, two girls and myself. He gave us each a little brush — but fluffier. Then he went away.

We looked at each other in wonder — except the Old Man. He said "Come on" and he led us down by the little River Blackwater, to the cucumber lines.

"This here's what you got t' do!"

He removed a cloche, brushed pollen from a male flower, and then brushed it into a female flower.

"We'm a fart'lizin ov 'em!" he said. "And dun't skimp it — else twun't be no good!" And he added dryly, "Dun't let it give yer no idears!"

No doubt it looked a bit odd. To see these intent stooping figures in line; removing cloches, fiddling about with the plants, putting them back, then on again . . .

And — it was the day of the Otter Hunt. I suppose there were about twenty people coming up by the river — a couple wading, and a handful of short-legged-looking hounds.

Most peculiar. All the hunters had thumbsticks. All — or nearly all were dressed in green. There were white-haired old ladies in thick green tweeds and ankle boots; bowler hatted men in tweed jackets and green aprons, and one with a tiny little horn in his hand.

Old Man Bungey glanced across — and his face went more expressionless than ever.

"Never mind *they* daft juggers!" he said. "Git on wi' what you're doing!"

Then one of the 'daft juggers', overcome by curiosity, broke off from the hunting-party and strolled up to the other side of the hedge. He leaned on his thumbstick, watching.

Old Man Bungey tensed, and kept his head down. And so did we . . .

At length, adressing himself to the Old Man, the otter-hunter called "My man!"

My man! Old Bungey tensed more than ever.

"My man!" called the otter-hunter again. "What exactly are you *doing?*"

Old Man Bungey slowly rose,and turned to face him. And he said, "We be 'atchin' otter eggs, Zur . . .!"

We were down in the greenhouses. I forget exactly what we were doing — stringing-up or something like that.

We *did* have proper lavatories of course. But they were down near the packing sheds. So if you were working in the fields up at the far end of the Nursery and you experienced a 'call' — well you looked round for somewhere a bit more handy. And the handiest place was — a long, narrow strip of copse, which divided two sets of fields . . .

On this day, there were some Land girls hoeing on one side of the coppice, and a bunch of our lads on the other. So they couldn't see each other.

We happened to notice one of the girls as she threw down her hoe. And turning from the hoeing party, she strolled over towards the strip. Almost at the same time, one of our lads threw down *his* hoe. And turning from *his* party, *he* strolled over towards the strip, too!

We all stopped work — fascinated. The Land girl went into the strip on her side, first. And our fascination grew as the lad started unbuttoning his trousers just before he entered on *his* side . . .

We didn't give a shout, or warn, or anything. We just looked . . .

And all of a sudden — out tore the Land Girl, screaming — we could hear her through the glass — pulling up her drawers as she ran! And out from the other side tore *our* lad, — doing up his flies . . .

There was a rush of orders. So it was week-end overtime. We were sat on our boxes in the packing-shed, snatching our sandwich lunches.

It was Sunday. So I suppose it was natural that our conversation should turn to religion . . .

"The Bible do contradict itself!" asserted Old Man Bungey.

"Look at that there story o' the Garden o' Heden. Adam were all on 'is own an' the Lard comes along an' 'e says, 'You looks a bit gloomy, old fellar.' 'Aye,' says Adam. 'I *be* a bit gloomy!'

"So the Lard decides to gie' un a companion to cheer un up. 'E dots Adam one on the chin to knock un out, takes out a rib, sticks a bit o' mud and plaster on it, breathes on it to come alive — and calls it ar' 'ooman'!

"Did ever you 'ear sech a tale in yer life! Anyways, 'twas the worst day's work the Lard ever done! 'Cause what did she do? Straightway," he said, "she bites old Adam's apple — an' that's where the trouble started! Dun't thee go bitin' nobody's apples my dear!" he said, turning to one of the Land Girls, "or you'll find yerself in the same 'ole as Eve did when *she* done it — in the Pudden Club!

"Anyways — she goes an 'as Cain and Abel. Now *'ere's* where the Bible d' contradict itself.

"It says that arter Cain bumped off Abel, 'e went off and found 'isself a wife in some foreign land. Well where did the wife come from? Tain't no use sayin' 'e got messin' abot wi *'apes* — 'cause I seen in the Daily Mail as we didn't come from no apes! It says *there* they've a-found the missin' link or summat — an' it weren't nar ape at all!

"So 'tis all wrong, ennit? 'Tis all wrong . . .!"

Alice was one of those motherly types who, wherever a group forms, automatically take-on the helpful background jobs. She brewed the tea, and washed-up the cups and saucers which the firm provided.

The girls' toilet was between the packing shed where we used to eat, and the office, where there was a bowl, a bucket of water, a towel and a primus stove.

I was a bit slow with my lunch one day — everyone else had gone back to the fields and the greenhouses. And I thought to myself, "I'm not going all over to the men's toilet! Nobody about — I'll pop in here!"

As I went to do so, the office door opened, and Alice appeared with an empty tray. She spotted my intention. "Hang on a minute!" she said.

She opened the toilet door, walked in, tugged on the chain. The old Victorian-style cistern rumbled and grumbled and discharged its contents. Alice stood staring down into the pedestal. Then she put the tray on the floor — and from out of the pedestal, all wet and shiny and washed — she retrieved our cups and saucers!

And said, as she bore them to the office to dry them "It's O.K. You can go now!"

I often wonder if it was at Shelley that I in fact saw the first prototype of the washing-up machine . . .!

JULY MORNING, 1974.

The footpath from Timsbury Waterworks to Michelmersh School.

I took Judy for a walk this morning. I thought perhaps she might refuse to come — seeing she had puppies in the shed. But she was quite pleased. She wobbled along with distended udders — like a miniature cow.

We went up the footpath behind the Waterworks. An elegant, mock-Gothic Victorian structure. A star of tall-windowed buildings, beautifully balanced. One of them *very* tall — where the old steam-pumps used to be. Converging to where, in the old days, a central square chimney-stack stood. And even that was architectured — broad at the base, and near the top high in the sky, sides slowly curving-in to a moulded lintel.

When they went over to diesel pumps, they took the stack down. I suppose they had to, really. But it's spoilt the whole thing. It still looks gracefully balanced — but rather decapitated. The tall pump-room isn't necessary now either. I suppose one day they will get a tame architect to come along and say that it's all of 'no architectural merit' — and down it will come, and we'll have instead the conventional box of the age.

Up on through the little coppice, and over the stile, and up through the field to the Brickyard. Kilns of the old bee-skip type still there, successfully converted to oil-fired — after a lot of worry and trial and error. Men in the making-sheds — dark shadows from here; a tall man taking lumps from the pug-mill, throwing them round to the tables. And the brickmakers — slap, bang, thud! — and slap, bang again, ever on the go like marionettes constantly jerked by strings. Hard, heavy, constant work; but the hand-brickmaker is a craftsman and you can keep him happy admiring what he does, and plying him with tea!

Over the little bridge where they used to haul-up clay loaded into the skip by hand, by a hand-turned winch. On past the worked-out area with its still, green pool in the bottom, and across the field at the top of Staff Road . . .

In the shade of the thickset hedge, all straggled and unkempt, — it had not been trimmed or laid for the past two or three years, — there stood giant candelabra, taller than myself, of the great yellow mulleins. Green candlesticks surmounted by a wide flame of light, yellow before the brambles.

A hissing curse exploded beside us in the air. I turned sharply, to see the fleeing ghost of the plover, flapping her sable wings. Back and forth, back and forth she went, seemingly erratically, dipping back to us almost frighteningly close at times, and crying desperately to her young ones to take the air. I knew they were about, because a month ago I saw one, just out of the egg. Suddenly, they took wing; still oddly marked, but sailing gracefully enough over the field away from us in the wake of their parent.

We went on down the road leading to Mesh, on the far side of Mottisfont Station. They were haymaking now; most of it cut and dry enough for the baler, while the weather still held. I saw one of these new

Opposite: "We passed into cool, soft light, beneath great curtains of green beech mast, and leaves soft with silver bloom. (Photograph: Robin Fletcher)

trailers on skids behind the baler, with a boy to load it. The bale was extruded from the machine in front straight on to this sledge, and the idea seemed to be to stack six bales across, with a seventh across them to anchor. But it seemed pretty evident that for this you needed a very smooth field. The sledge lurched and bumped over uneven ground, and there were frequent stoppages to pick-up bales which had fallen off.

Barley, barley everywhere — the ecological and conservationist prophets of doom over continuous monoculture ignored while the cash rolls in. It is used to feed animals now kept off the fields. They tell us this is a 'must' if we are to continue to supply food to our ever-increasing population.

But there is always the huge problem of what to do with the effluents from these factory farms. In some places they make huge lagoons of it — and hope it will not eventually soak through the earth to contaminate our water-supplies. My neighbouring farmer solves his problem by spreading it in liquid form on the fields. When he does this, the pong through the village is terrifying. Everyone rushes to close windows and doors in vain effort to keep it out. When you do that it certainly seems to keep it out of the bottom of the house — but it *does* seep in and creep off upstairs to greet you when you go to bed!

Generally he treats us to this effluvia just after he returns from his holidays. One villager told him in his Club — "Oh I knew you was back — soon as I could smell dung!"

All along the hedges were masses of little yellow rock-roses. I saw a partridge family, with young not much larger than chicks, but quite able to fly. Some say *they* are dying-out. The baby chicks are entirely dependent on light insects; and these are put paid to by chemical sprays.

The cock pheasant hurled himself from the verge couch-grass with a cry of alarm, wings whirring as he sailed towards the beeches, just clearing the tops, then gliding on down the other side.

On one farm, they were just putting the finishing touches to a silage, or green-grass stack. I did not like the way they were doing it. They were compressing a huge heap by running a tractor up one end and down the other. But as the tractor neared the sides, it tipped alarmingly. I thought the driver was mad — I wouldn't have taken chances like that! But they got away with it and put a plastic sheet over, and weighted it down with old motor-car tyres.

We passed into cool, soft light, beneath great curtains of green beech-mast, and leaves soft with silver bloom. A little further on, a very old lady was busy with shears, trimming her hedge. She said she was well, except for a touch of blood-pressure which had 'gone off' now. She was making a very good job of the hedge.

Judy was beginning to pant. So it was time for a rest. We went into a field where the verge bracken was shoulder high. Someone had backed into it, and emptied sump-oil. But you could still smell the pure, earthy scent of crushed bracken, rather like wild mushrooms.

We found a spot further on, and sat in the bracken, in the shade. We heard the pigeons in the high tree-tops — 'I *do* know Billy! I *do* know Billy! I *do* know Billy — yes!' We heard the endless song of the lark — and a thrush over the near copse. More long beech-festoons and curtains over there — and a second crop of oak-leaves — the lammas-crop — yellow green, to replace those eaten by a plague of caterpillars earlier in the year. Yew-shoots, bright against the darker canopy. And even yet, late in the morning as it now was, dew in the shade, held in the seed-heads of the grass, like little pools of cotton-wool blue . . .

Zummer be come __
weather be voine.
Grass 'opper zings in blaze.
Barley be dry —
wheat-'eads milky.
Ripples on wutts do reace.

Daisy d' stare —
bindweed d' blaw.
Buttervly dances, look!
Dogrose be out —
thistles d' zeed.
Foxglove be stood b' brook.

Bracken grows tall —
poppy do weep.
Bittersweet vlowers 'angs down.
Pimpernel eyes
all reddled d' shaw.
Old dog do pant, and frown.

Yere, Judy-gal —
out o' thic heat!
'Tis zent-down too 'ard vor thee!
Coom on in sheade
unner the weed!
bide yere in cool — wi' me!

THE COUNTY LIMP

Sandy stood looking through the Malt House bar window. He was a man in his seventies — but a *young* man in his seventies. Argumentative. Pugnacious. A rough old tough old relic of the old navvying days. But as everybody knew, a ministering slave to his invalid wife . . .

At one time, he had a shock of red hair. And the pale, freckled complexion that went with it.

But now, the hair beneath his cloth cap, still worn at a jaunty angle, was as white as his bushy brows and his bristling moustache. And the pale complexion had become permanently ruddy . . .

His white old brows lowered as he stood there. His red old face registered deep disgust.

"Luk at un!" he said. "Wavin' t' they old wimmin! That's about all 'e's cut-out far. The fat, lazy gert thing!"

We knew at once who he was on about. Tommo Gunner, the roadman . . .

Sandy placed the side of his face neaerer the window so that he could squint down as far as the Causeway.

"Luk at un! Do you know 'ow long he ben workin' up from the Causeway there — not more 'n two 'unnerd yard?"

Nobody knew.

"Two days" said Sandy. "Two days! That's as true as I got this yere pint pot in my 'and! *Two days* t' trim-off two 'unnerd yard! And for what 'e *'ave* a-trimmed off — unless you seen un there, you ha' thought 'e 'adn't a-been! What's think 'o *that,* then?"

Nobody thought anything.

"And you knows why 'e 'angs about there — dun' 'ee?"

Nobody knew that either.

"Because," said Sandy, his face redder than ever and his blue eyes ferociously gleaming, "'E's 'opin' somebody 'll be daft enough to take pity on un — and buy un a pint! You see! Every time they old wimmin comes along — out comes 'is 'andkercher and 'e d' wipe that gert broad fore'ead o' his 'n as got nothen be'ind it and 'e d' say, '*Thirsty* work Missus! *Thirsty* work.''

It seemed Sandy's tirade was thirsty work too. He took a great gulp from his beer-mug, wiped his moustache with the back of his hand, and came back to the bar.

"I got no time for un!" he said.

That we *did* know.

Do you know 'ow 'e got that job?" he said, fixing us again with a fierce blue eye. "'E went down the Labour, and they put un on the Council. 'E was took-on as mate. 'E 'ad to empt they lorries as carries gert pipes and curbstones and such. Waal 'e didn't go much on that, so 'e goes sick. Bad back. Gets 'isself a Doctor's cusstificate to say 'e couldn't lift.

"So they says to un — did 'e think 'e could use ar shovel? Ah — 'e expects 'e could — long as it warn't too big! So they gie un a shovel an' put en on spreadin' grit be'ind the tar. That was all right for a fartnight. Then 'e comes 'obblin' to work one marnen' wi' rheumaticks in the knee.

"Not 'is *left* knee look. 'Is *right* knee! So 'e couldn't push the shovel under the grit! It did 'urt 'is knee too much!"

He drained his pot, thumped it on the bar and looked for the Landlord.

"Where is 'er?"

"Settin' up the barrels," somebody said.

"Waal," he said. "That's what they calls the 'County Limp'! If you cain't *lift* nothen, nor push nar shovel — well what *can* you do? You can only trim-up the grass alonzid the road wi' a hook. So they gies un a stretch o' road — and makes un a roadman!"

"O' course," said Sandy, "they as gets the job like that got to go on limpin' for rest o' their lives! But they soon gets into the way on 't. But that's 'ow Tommo got *'is* job! The old County Limp!"

The Landlord returned.

"*You* takes yer time!" said Sandy.

"If you can do it quicker — you're welcome!" said the Landlord.

He refilled Sandy's mug.

Sandy strolled back to the window. We watched as he resumed his study of the object of his contempt.

"Come 'ere!" he said.

Nobody moved.

"Come an 'ave a look!"

I moved over to Sandy's side.

"'E's comin' over look! I bet you 'e don't come in!"

I watched Tommo as he looked carefully up the road, then down the road, and then crossed towards us. He got as far as the Malt House sign. Sure enough, he stopped, and stared. The brass buckle on his broad leather belt holding up his corduroy trousers, gleamed in the sun.

He turned round. He looked carefully down the road, then up the road, and went back to his task again. He stared across the opposite fields as he expertly flicked at the blade of his hook with his bluestone.

"Never did I see a blade sharpened so much as 'ad such little to cut," said Sandy, sourly. "D'you know why 'e didn't come in?"

I didn't know why he didn't come in.

"'E zid my bike!" said Sandy.

I went back, smiling, to the bar.

"Tell me Sandy — why have you got it in for Tommo so?"

He came away from the window and leaned an elbow on the bar. Again he fixed me with a fierce blue eye.

"I'll tell 'e," he said.

"When 'e first tuk-on the job o' Roadman luk, 'e used to come trimmin' up round our back lanes — 'cause that was part o' the job. An' 'e took 'is time. I never knowed un do more 'n ten yard in a day — hafe as much agen if you were lucky.

"I knowed what 'e was up to. 'E didn't want to work 'is way down on to the main road where 'e might be zid, no quicker 'n 'e could 'elp. 'Cause y' see they might come out from the Council Office along the main road. But they never come up the lanes.

"Waal — I wasn't worried about *that* — though I don't reckon much on payin' taxes for nothen, like anybody else. But what got up *my* back was this.

"'E'd go messin' and messin' around the Vicarage 'edge and trim it all up for the Parson, — which 'e'd no right to do, — and spend as long agen messin' and messin' round old Farmer Cross's 'edge, too! And there was one or two others 'e done that wi'. But when 'e come down to *our* little places — 'e never put 'ook to bank! We 'ad to go out and do our own!

"So I says to un one day, 'Look yere, roadman! What's the idea o' messin' and messin' round the Parson's hedge and old Farmer Cross's and places like that — an leavin ourn?'

"'Oh!' 'e says. 'You always *'ave* a-done yourn!'

"'Ho no we ain't!' I says.

"Ho yes you ave!' says 'e — and off 'e goes!

"Well," said Sandy. "I didn't like that, look. So I let *my* front go— 'cause I ain't the sort o' man as gives in.

"Then it come later in the year — and I was diggen taters. An' up alonzid the heidge come old Tommo.

"'Hyup.' he says. I didn't take no notice. 'E stood about there, and 'e says,

"'You got some good taters there then Sandy'. I says 'Yes, I know'.

"I still took no notice on un look, and 'e was makin' 'isself comfortable like wi' 'is foot on 'is shovel, starin' round wi' that daft look 'e got about un. So I says,

"'Ain't you got nuthen better to do?'

"'What d'ye mean?' 'e says.

"I says 'What I says'. If you ain't got nuthen t' do — you can dig out the ditch in front o' my heidge there — an' trim that there verge as you ain't touched for the past year!'

"'Hugh! 'e says. 'I got no time to do that!'

"'Well!' I says. 'You got time to 'ang round the Vicarage for the odd 'alf-crown — and old Farmer Cross's as gie's 'e a pint if you catches un in Malt 'ouse, aint ye?'

"'Hugh!' 'e says. 'If *that's* 'ow you be — I'd best get on!'

"I says 'Yes you *'ad! I* got plenty t' do if *you* ain't!

"Waal," said Sandy, "I might ha' done n' more! But 'twas my nipper's motor-car!

"Now we didn't 'ave nar garage nor nothen like that, so nipper, 'e used to pull-in 'is car hafe off the lane on to the verge, and let un stand there o' nights. Waal — nobody comed up much — so 'e never left no side-lights on.

"And then, one day, — a little bit arter this here affair, — I seen th'old copper a-comen up our garden path.

"Allo!' I says. 'What do *you* want?' And 'e says,

"'Now don't you get on at *me* Sandy — and don't think 'tis arn o' *my* doin' — 'cause it ain't! But I've 'ad instructions to come and tell you that if your nipper's going to leave 'is car alongside the lane at nights — 'e must 'ave 'is lights on! Either that — or it must be right off the road altogether."

"So I says to un, 'Do you know 'ow long my nipper's been puttin' 'is car there? *Three years!* Whoever gie you they instructions — it took 'em a hell of a long time to find out about it — didn't it?'

"'Can't 'elp that, Sandy!' he said. 'They *'ave* a-found out — and that's it!'

"'And who told 'em?' I says.

"'Ah!' says the copper. 'I cain't tell ye that!' So I says to un

"'Well I'll tell *thee!* 'Twas a gert, fat, lazy good-for-nuthen as wanders up and down yere now and agen wi' a 'ook in 'is 'and, and spends all 'is time talkin' to the old gals over their 'edges as puts hafe-a-crown in 'is pocket doin' odd jobs for 'em — when 'e's *s'posed* to be ditchen' — and trimmin' the verge!'

"But the old copper 'e jes laughed — and went on!"

Sandy paused, drank half-way down his mug, keeping his blue eyes fixed on me meanwhile. Then again wiping his moustache, he went on,

"Course — I wadn't goin' to put up wi' that! So I ups on me old bike — and away I goes to the Council Offices. I see the man as looks to the roads — old Mr Plum. And I asks un,

"When's old Tommo Gunner goin' to trim-up the verge outside my cottage?' And 'e says,

"'It's been done — hasn't it?' I says

"'Have you been out to see?' So he says,

"'Well we can't be *everywhere* at once — but I'll come out.'

So when 'e came, I showed 'im my place, and all the other little places Tommo 'd a-left. And then I showed un the Vicarage 'edge. And 'ow old Tommo 'd ha' trimmed-up for Farmer Cross.

"Waal — come next day, up come old Tommo. 'E was real *nasty* — I could see that! 'E flipped along our verge in about two minutes and then went away past old Mrs Head's and on down by the Blacksmith's — and there 'e stuck. 'E never did nar another stroke for the rest o' the day.

"So when 'e'd a-gone I went out to 'ave a look. Trim? You couldn't 'ardly see where 'e'd a-ben! 'Twarn't all that different from afore 'e come along!

"So!" said Sandy. "Do you know what I done? I went out along the lane, and I picked up all the trimmin's as 'e'd ha cut for the day! And do you know what? I could 'old em all — *all* ov 'em — in *one 'and!*"

Sandy's hand was held dramatically before him, grasping an imaginary handful of weeds.

"*One 'and!* So back I goes to the Council Offices and Mr Plum wadn't there — so I seen the General Foreman.

"'Yere!' I says — and I 'eld out this yere bunch o' trimmin's under 'is nose!' 'Do you know what *this* is Cecil?'

"'E says 'Ah! Bunch o' weed!' I says,

"'*Tis* a bunch o' weed!' And I'll tell thee what *else* it is! 'Tis *one man's work — for one whole day!*' And I told un all about it!"

Sandy paused.

"Well what did the Foreman say to that then?"

Sandy took a deep breath. He was more flushed than ever.

"He didn't say nuthen! 'E didn't seem all that much concerned! So I says 'Look yere, Cecil! I don't pay taxes for *noth'n!* What you gwine t' *do* about it?'

"'What am I goin' to *do* about it?' 'e says. 'What *can* I do? I cain't speak arsh to un — can I?'

"Ah!" said Sandy, his moustache bristling with the memory of it all. "That's what 'e said — 'I cain't speak *'arsh* to un! If I does that,' 'e said ''e might chuck 'is 'and in?'

"Chuck 'is 'and in?' I says. 'What do *that* matter? 'E cain't do less than noth'n at all! Well — if *you* cain't speak 'arsh to un,' I says, 'I shall ha' to get 'old o' somebody as will!'

"'Oh all right Sandy,' 'e says, 'All right — don't be too 'asty — I'll see what I can do!'

"So you see," said Sandy, "They took un off the back lanes and put un down on the main road where they can keep an eye on un! They've brought in the next lengthman along to do our lane — and 'e gen'lly does mine first!"

Again Sandy's blue eyes ferociously gleamed.

"Why *should* we ratepayers pay out good 'apence to save the likes o' the Parson and old Farmer Cross puttin' their 'ands in their pockets for to pay a man proper to do their work? Why *should* we?"

"Why indeed?" I said.

Sandy drank up his pint, banged the mug down on the bar, shouted 'Good-Day' to the Landlord who was back in the cellar again and did not reply, and was gone.

I saw him push his bicycle across the front yard of the Inn, tramping purposefully upon those bandy legs of his. I saw him pause, cock his hat over his eyes, and look in Tommo's direction.

Tommo kept a broad back stoutly towards him. But when Sandy got on his way, Tommo looked after him — and spat in the dust.

Then he put down his bluestone and his trimming hook. He looked up the road, and then down the road, crossed to the Inn Sign, and came in.

He was one of those slow-moving, lethargic, yet immensely powerful Westcountrymen — brown as a berry.

"Thirsty work guv'nor!" he said, sinking down on the settle. "Days like this, doost d' get in the throat summat cruel!"

He rummaged about in his waistcoat pockets. Then he said,

"I dun't want nobody to take nuth'n the wrong way, guv'nor, — but *your heidge!*"

"My hedge?"

"Ah! You bein' on the carner-like. It d' stick-out too far thee's knaw! Folk cain't see round in their motor-cars when they turns up into Waterworks Road!"

"Oh can't they? I've never noticed that!"

"Ah — that's cause you be with un all the time luk! But 'e *do* stick out! You'll be gettin' a letter from the Council if you don't look-out!"

"Oh! We don't want that!"

"No! " said Tommo. He gave up rummaging in his waistcoat pockets and tried the back pocket of his corduroys.

"I'll tell thee what," he said, "Save any bother. When I comes down-along your way, 'touldn't be no odds to me for to lift my 'ook a little bit 'igher!"

"Wouldn't it, Tommo? Are you *sure*?"

"'Twould't be so *expensive* neither! As payin' out a chap special for to do it!"

I said, "Tommo — what are going to have?"

He stopped rummaging.

"Oh! Kind on 'e, Guvnor! Pint o' the best bitter? If I bain't askin' too much?"

"Course not!" I said, and turned to the bar. But the pint of best bitter was already drawn-up and standing there!

"Thanks Guv'nor!" said Tommo.

He drank deeply.

"'*Tis* thirsty work!" he said. "Doost d' get in the throat summat cruel!

AUGUST MORNING 1970
"Ma's World"

When Mother-in-Law died, she had almost reached the age of ninety.

She did not want to die. She wasn't afraid. She was just interested in life; in the village, her Club, in us all — and it was all *that* she didn't want to leave.

And she wouldn't be left out. She grumbled a great deal at her increasing frailty towards the end. Not because of illness itself — but because it stopped her — from doing her share.

Or so she thought. How much she contributed, even when she could hardly move from her chair by the window, we did not fully realise, until we had to do it for ourselves . . .

The gooseberries used to be picked — and passed in to Ma. She'd top and tail them for wine or jam — with a pair of nail scissors! We would rough pick the fruit; blackberries, strawberries, blackcurrants — and pass them in to Ma. And out they would come, clean as a whistle for whatever we wanted to do with them.

She would de-stone the damsons and the plums. Peel and core the apples for pies and bottling. Peel the shallots and the spuds — the dozens of nit-picking, time-consuming jobs country folk do — or *did* do — for cooking, preserving and so forth. She was still at them up to a week or so before she died. In her sleep, thank God!

So I took over her room for my office. And naturally, I have my table and typewriter before her window. The window she spent hours peering out of and never missed a thing of what was going on outside . . . I had the strange feeling, and still do, that I had inherited with Ma's window, Ma's world . . .

(1) The Storm 13.8.79 11 am

Wisped, bleached ghosts of shucked grass-seed stems, bob helplessly on the green, before the gale. Flaming ragweed, jostled and shoved. Purple plumes of swaying thistles. Plantain heads like swimmers struggling in a wild surge of weed. Hoary-headed wild carrot bunched and stumbled together, and the shelter of lilac scabious rudely swept aside.

Smouldering agrimony hopelessly entwined. Tall stems of hogweed with their plates of seed on outstretched fingers, swinging. Together with dry-leafed, insect-holed nettles. Ceaselessly back and forth, back and forth . . .

Hazel and elder, with leaves turned inside-out, turn swaying coppice flanks from green to silver. Branch-ends of maple turn back upon themselves, and bob, and sway. Dark and sturdy oaks growl their displeasure. But the rigid hawthorn acknowledges the gale not at all.

Great weights of ash-leaves and seed-bunches are swept up and turned back down-wind. The spread of giant leaves are like petticoats blown inside out, covering the smaller greens, and so protecting all.

In the border outside, pansies flutter. And marigolds bob jerky, yellow-red heads.

Few birds chance the gale — there are none on the green at feed. The odd swift makes a tippling, erratic, side-slipping, barley controlled pencilled appearance, across rolled grey-and-white tumbling clouds. A visitor blown off-course from the hills, beak gripped firmly upon some grassland creepy-

69

crawly, grabs at a rock-garden stone to stay its headlong flight. It bows, calls 'chack, chack!' — how birds do that with their beaks stuffed I've never found out! — then bobs and bows its way from couch-hummock to hummock, until it is blown under the barbed wire into the fields again. I have to think for a bit. I know — a stonechat! Migrating. August is the month for its going.

Rooks, perhaps five or six, launch raggedly from the oak-tree head. They are deflected down — down. Pressed firmly by an invisible hand down into Geoffrey Pratt's fields.

Through wall and window, so that the house seems to vibrate to it, the multiple voice of the coppice in tumult. Hissing anger of hazel and willows. Oak trees' rumble, and sudden roar. A noise like a train approaching. A huge increase in coppiceland confusion and consternation, like the clash and screech of pebbles tumbled on the beach before a raging sea . . .

Fleeting sun. Cloud shadows running in cross-country marathon one behind the other. Down hills, across the green — faster, faster than the swiftest athlete, be he man or hare . . .

And yet, miraculously, wee gauze helicopters of hoverflies remain poised over rock-garden shrubs and flowers, in the face of it all. And bees go about their business as if nothing extraordinary is happening at all. Shrill 'seep' from wren. Otherwise from the woodland birds — no sound.

Not Ma's weather. At times like this, the curtains would be drawn and on would go the 'telly'. With a bit of worry of course, in case the ariel blew down!

It is fashionable to scoff at people who turn-on the Television first thing, and leave it flickering away until close-down time. 'Wasting' hours of precious life, mesmerised before it.

You wait until you're old. Perhaps on your own. Perhaps unable to get about any more. Or maybe not able to read — even with specs . . .

(2) The Aftermath. 14.8.79. 7 a.m.

The Fastnet yacht race blown to pieces. Twenty-seven rescued so far. Ten drowned, seven unaccounted for. One hundred and thirty-seven yachts so far missing . . .

To look through Ma's window this morning, it seems impossible that all this could have happened yesterday.

All is peace and quiet. A blue sky, cloudless sky, a burnished horizon. A vast multitude of glistening green mirrors, reflecting from the kale fields the light of the morning sun.

Long, long copseland shadows across the green almost from one side to the other. The hand of Nature's year-long clock, pointing already towards autumn.

A thrush, — or is it? — busy on soaked soil just outside the window, between pansies and marigolds still closed in sleep. Its bill is thick with mud. It wipes it clean on a creeper-cushion. Then carries on dibbling again, one round eye all the time focussed on me.

A chaffinch, attracted by its activity, flits down to the rose-stump. Immediately the 'thrush' — which I can now see is too dark for a thrush and is in fact a young blackbird similarly marked, — glances up. The chaffinch is warned off.

Suddenly there is a "pop-pop-pop-pop-pop!" A stuttering to life of a chain-saw. The modern woodman cutting-down his hazel wands.
(Photograph: James Smith)

A small, thin-billed, pale-breasted with faint striations, nondescript grey little bird, rather upright, — one of the warblers perhaps, — also turns-up, fractionally. But it also makes-off at the blackbird's threat.

A ballet is in progress on the far side of the green. The performers — upright, thrust-bosomed, long-necked common gulls. They glide through bars of sunlight-and-shadow, with the swift, splay-footed goose-walk of ballerinas. They group on this side of the stage, then the other. Endlessly moving; now in pairs, now in threes. Now a chorus, all meandering swiftly in tight circles, occasionally flashing a beak to the ground. It seems more of a social than a feeding performance.

In the midst of it, the rook is busy, — but wary, — shovelling the soil. Another busies itself in mud between the far goalposts.

The young blackbird just outside is now over the bank and on the lawn just below the windowsill. It is more upright now. A well-shouldered bird, carefully studying the white human face staring at it from the window. It stops and starts, then becomes bolder. Like the robin, the blackbird soon recognises the human who is not going to interfere with it.

So it hops into the grass silvered by dew, almost as high as its breast. Each time its tail touches wetness, it is flicked up out of it; blackbird's don't really like the damp.

Suddenly it dives. An enormous worm is hauled half-out from the soil. There is a colossal tussle. The worm swells itself tight into its hole, the blackbird heaves mightily. The worm yields — and off goes the bird with its weighty, squirming burden, into the copse.

Cloud-towers grow upwards from the valley's far rim, then lean upon each other and slowly glide eastwards. Dabbled shadow on the road beyond the rock-garden begins to gently move. Sheep do not settle. There is movement all along the copse edge, and a long, despairing sigh as if to say 'Is it all going to happen again?'

Suddenly there is a 'pop-pop-pop-pop! Pop-pop-pop-pop! — and then the stuttering to life of a chain-saw in the copse depth, like a motor-bike with its exhaust fallen off. It is the sound of the modern woodsman cutting down the hazel wands.

The wood-birds don't like that. They flit silently through the branches away from the scene. Far different from the old days when all you heard was the chip-chip-chop! of the hand-hook. Or the distinctive tearing sound of the hurdle-maker splitting his wands, while the birdsong went on around him unabated.

The noise disturbs the ballet, which sweeps en masse towards the backdrop of the stage, — a long hawthorn hedge, a brick Jubilee bus-stop and a line of sloping bungalow roofs on the other side of the road.

A great prop moves along the back of the stage behind the hedge and in front of the bungalows, with the word TESCO written upon it. The ballet sweeps forward again. Another prop moves along the same route but going the opposite way, bearing the words CARPET EXPRESS. It is all too much for the ballet Company, which now vanishes silently into the wings.

Martins take their places with almost butterfly-like movements. Quartering the green as the sun rises, the shadows shorten, and the warmth brings up insects from the ground.

The angled paralleogram of the far goal-posts gleams up white in the sun. Folk back their cars out into the road, and move off on their ways to work. Villagers come down to run their dogs and foul the green. Old Willie Garland goes cycling up the hill. My wife and neighbours' wives are out to look for new flowers in their front gardens. And to pull a weed or so before starting the morning's chores . . .

All this Mother-in-law saw from her window. It still goes on, — Ma's world . . .

I wonder if some day someone will be looking out of this window after I am gone, seeing much the same. And perhaps saying,

"I have the strange feeling that I have inherited with Dad's window, *Dad's* world . . ."

72

Country Character

Have all the old 'characters' of the countryside gone? Are they curious figures of the past, whose like we shall never see again?

I don't know. 'Characters' — are people who are remembered. They emerge — when you think back. You go down to the local or your Club and you say,

"Do you remember little Frankie Ephamy?" And your friend replies,

"Oh ah! There was nothing of him! He was like a rasher of wind!"

Then you tell what you remember of Frankie, and that triggers your friend. He goes and tells others — and *they* remember things. And so a 'character' is born . . .

But note your friend's reply 'Oh ah! There was nothing of him! He was like a rasher o' wind!' Surely, by the way he expresses himself, — *he* has 'character' too! Why don't you notice it? Because he is familiar.

But he *will* be remembered. Someone in years to come will remember his turn of speech, and recall it, and many other things about him when, through death, he is familiar no more . . .

My Grandfather was born at Crewkherne. He came to take up his post as Stationmaster at the now defunct Mottisfont Station in Hampshire, nearly seventy years ago. There are still people in my village who remember him. People whose family names can be seen in our Parish records of *three hundred* years ago. And they might still say — trying to place me, — "Oh ah! You come up from *Somerset* — didn't ye?"

I didn't. I was born *here* — in Hampshire. And so were some of my Aunts. But what these village ancients meant by *"You"* — was not me specially, but my whole family tribe.

When I was compiling notes with the help of my North Hampshire foster-father for a book I was writing about the Basingstoke area, I said, "Let's see. The Goodenoughs are *Baughurst* people — aren't they?"

"Baughurst!" he said. "They bain't *Baughurst!* They be *Lunnoners!"* And it was all of half a century previous to this that they came !

So it was a long, long apprenticeship in those days — before you were accepted!

And the New Foresters — well — they were their own race! Rarely, if ever, would they let you know them on their own ground! But you could catch them with their hair down at the Angel in Romsey, the pub near the Market. That was held on Thursdays. Well on in the afternoon was the best time to catch them. When their faces were red, and they are admitting to each other how they had swindled each other rotten! They never rowed about it. The one who'd been 'done' would say "Well — my turn'll come, you old jugger!" And he made sure it did.

That was how country 'character' was — or as I found it anyway.

Is it still so? No — not like *that* any more, because they belonged to their day. There might still be the old oddity who sticks out like a sore thumb among all the people who have moved into his village from the town. He is a 'character' of course — but he doesn't belong to *our* day.

Here's a little tip. When you come out to the country pub — don't go sitting in the lounge all the time, giving yourself airs, talking about the job and those eternal motor-cars — which after all, are so like each other these days that there's no longer any 'character' about them at all! Creep off round to the public bar — round about, say ten o'clock.

There will be your locals, young and old, starting to let their hair down! *Then* you'll hear it all — blowing-up as strong as ever! The old country cracks — "Thee cassn't zee so well as thee coulds't, — cas't?" "Mind thee pin-bone, Missus! You got en up agin the shove 'apenny-board — and you'm pushen it all thicways an athirt!"

Everybody will roar.

But the *real* joke will be that after they have so deliberately parodied themselves to make *you* laugh — they'll go on talking much like that — without even knowing it!

So there's still country *character* about — if there's fewer country characters! And I think if it can survive the bashing it has received from the influx of 'furriners' over the past few decades so far — it very likely always *will* be about! And thank goodness for that!

Hallo, the milking-herd is out!   *(Photograph: James Smith)*

SEPTEMBER MORNING, 1979
Timsbury, the Village Green.

Come up to the window. Gently. Not too close . . .

That corner of the Green across the road, where the grasscutter turns and it's always left, — it's like a little garden. Seeds of parsley and yarrow. Plates of hogweed tilted away from the copse on dusty fingers — all hardened by the sun . . .

Ragweed still smouldering its gold in the shadow. Hardhead fluffs. Thistle plumes, bleached-blue now, and there's musk, and the red-brown stems and seeds of sorrel. The grass-heads dry-white, seeds gone, empty.

See that? Perhaps not — too fast! A jenny-wren fractionally lodged on that ivy-stem. Gone now — into the undergrowth. It's so tiny — to keep alive it has to keep feeding all the time. An endless search for insects and fallen seed . . .

In the copse, it's still dark. Dark in the shadow beyond the weed-tangle — but lightening all the time . . .

There look! Three dark, upright figures — about a foot-and-a-half high! About ten yards from the coppice edge. Spaced equally apart.

Rabbits. Perfectly still. Angled away from us, for flight. Three single eyes, focussed on the window from the sides of three heads, — ears upright, and rigid!

No sense in hiding — they know we're here! But we shall have to be careful. Quiet, easy movements — I'll just open the window from the side, to get a better view . . .

There! Three eyes still rivetted, — unblinking. That one nearest the copse is angling itself to a flight-line directly towards the tangle under the hazels.

They're still not moving. They're still not relaxed. We shall have to wait . . .

Ah — the far one's put its ears down! It's humping its back — it's nibbling the grass! The one nearest the copse isn't so sure. See — it's turned round to look with the other eye! The one in the middle stays rigid . . .

They've decided we're harmless! Toilet-time for the middle one, — it's almost like a cat! Back leg lifted forwards, turning its head to nibble its paw. Perhaps trimming its claws — or washing its foot — the grass is still damp after last night's storm. Their coats are all matted because of the damp, too . . .

Look — just like a cat — it's licking over its shoulder! Now scratching the back of its neck, — I expect it's infested with fleas.

It's spotted something! Bolt upright on its haunches, feet held like a squirrel, ears upright again, — a statue!

The other two are feeding — but not very enthusiastically. I've got an idea they don't like the wet. That one nearest the copse — as it moves in it goes darker, like a chameleon. If we hadn't been watching, we'd never have known it was there! I *wondered* about that bare patch along the copse edge! Now we can see why!

Rabbits *can* run look — *I* thought they only hopped! A bit ungainly — a sort of short-foreleged-long-backlegged run, and then they turn to nibble at the edge of the bare patch.

That far rabbit's off down to the end of the copse. A blackbird hops out from the corner. The rabbit runs round him. They're both side-by-side. And both — still keeping a sharp eye on our window!

There are other shapes now, — running on the turf. Small, dark ones. Blackbirds — one, two, three, — now four, — five! That's because of the storm early in the night. But I expect the pickings are still hard — before last night there hasn't been any rain for a month!

They're quiet. Not much bird-song.

How do I *know* they're blackbirds? When you get to know, you can tell distant birds in a bad light by the way they move. A bold run forward, instant peck; pause, change direction, run forward again, — that's the blackbird.

The nearest one's seen us! Warning rattle — long-angled flight up into the hazels. The Great Spotted Woodpecker answering from somewhere inside — birds know each others' warning calls. The others just pause, then run, then pause, and peck again. I suppose they feel safer because they're further away.

There's a long, slimmer shape just beyond them. Shorter, swifter runs — not much direction-changing. Head up, longer pauses. A swift 'dart' — rather than a peck. Head up, pause again, — short, swift run.

That's the lapwing. You can see it anyway, as the light strengthens. White breast, and from here its back seems a delicate, pencilled grey. Sudden beautiful angel-wing flash of sable and wing underwhite. Oh yes — that's the lapwing; unmistakeable in her little cocked hat!

There's a *thrush* look! Upright, pale-breasted. It moves *like* a blackbird — but takes longer runs. A less bold, less vigorous pecking . . .

There's a magpie school on the green's far edge; a black-and-white, fearless bustle . . .

The dew seems to be thickening. Where the grass was brown — it all turns grey-green. Through it, the stout, upright, confident black-giant waddle of the crow — black to the root of its bill. Not much for him I shouldn't think. No — he's off. I didn't think he'd stay long . . .

Look! Burst-out from under the far fence like a big sandhopper — that brown-grey, rangy figure! Fast-moving, erratic. Flick-flick this way, — flick-flick that way! Curled-up suddenly in that one spot in a furry ball! Ears laid along its back, — suddenly cocked, — very long! Long, stringy, kicking-back legs — more erratic springing, this way, that way — even sideways!

There's another! *Two* of them springing here, there, everywhere, — but keeping around the field-edge where they came from!

You're right — they are young hares.

The unmistakeable waddle of the wood-pigeon. And how's that for impudence — one fluttered down in front of us, right into the road outside! Rippling his old vinegar-breast in the sunrise. Grey-blue coated and white-collared, pecking for grit with his fleshy old beak, — just as it we weren't there!

I'll bet that's the one who pecks at my cabbage-plants! If I had an airgun or catapult and caught him at it — well — I would probably do nothing! A love-hate relationship you see!

A beautiful bird. And me? A frustrated, mildly dangerous provider of cabbages! And just to rub it in — he's sitting there look, puffing his throat and *telling* us "I *see* you! I *see* you! I *see* you! Yes!"

The poor little robin humped on the rose-stump — you can hardly recognise him. Moulting, ragged miserable — you can only just see the red smudge on his breast!

Long shadows on the cricket-pitch for a few moments, — then they are gone. It's the dew condensed into mist. The shadows will be back soon — then they'll stay.

Let's have a cup of tea . . .

The shadows are back — it's going to be a fine day. It's odd, that as daylight strengthens, it warms-up at first, then for half-an-hour or so it suddenly cools, and then warms-up again . . .

The magpies have gone into the copse. I don't think they'd touch the woodpecker — but he doesn't sound very pleased! Listen — little thin voices of wagtails out there on the Green — but too far off to be properly seen . . .

Hallo — the milking-herd is out. Making its leisurely way up the far slope facing the sun. I know the routine — I was once a dairyman myself. They'll be sluicing-down the holding-yards by the milking-bale just now, before going in for breakfast. The sheep huddle together as the herd passes by . . .

A flock of lapwings moving in high from the coast. The ones on the green give no sign. One or two straggling flocks of gulls. Perhaps the fine weather won't hold then? They usually start coming in when it's rough on the coast.

There — down by the far goalposts! A large, tubby, pearl-backed, black-headed, white-breasted very upright lad — or lass — the black-headed gull. All alone — so not at ease. Legs so short you can't see them moving — it seems to sail across the grass just as it would in water. On grass it always moves in a meandering series of circles, very tight. It doesn't seem to find much. It won't stay long . . .

The sky's brightening just behind the ash-tree. Great compound, narrow-lobed, pointed, long, still leaves, bowed with sleep and dampness. I've noticed at nights that all less rigid leaf-growth above ground tends to fold *downwards*. All nearest the ground — like kale — fold upwards. If you look under the ash branch-stems, you'll see the big seed-bunches like hanging baskets. On the edge of the copse they're turning yellow-brown. brown.

The maple stems, — over there, poking through the ivy, — are all green with lichen and algae. It's always pretty damp if you live near a copse. Maple leaves are a bit similar in shape to the ivy; both five-lobed. From here it's a job to tell them apart, — except that the maple's beginning to turn. The maple branches always in shadow have begun to die-off.

You can see the wagtails now — flitting back-and-forth on the cricket-pitch. Sandmartins — a bit late — still about; following the insects between the tree-tops. They come down to within inches of the Green. That's because the Green is warming-up. The insects dry-out, so they can fly, and start rising. There's a little wee gauze helicopter up already — just beyond the corner of the window!

Old vinegar-breast is still at it in the road! Oh — *that's* done it! Out goes our old black walking hearth-rug, Jesse! No — *I* don't know what breed she is! A bit of Poodle mixed up in her somewhere! Her first job every morning is to amble out and roll in the middle of the road!

Vinegar-breast takes-off. He goes up in a long, curved glide, like an early Voisin pre-1918 flying-machine. Dips, claps his wings, and there he is on top of the ash-tree, looking back at Jesse in disgust!

As if *she* cares! Rolling joyously on her back — her black paws threshing the air . . .!

77

Well — that's the end of the Show! Our morning actors have now melted from the Green, and it's now empty. It will remain so for the rest of the day — except for human beings and their dogs.

Next curtain-up, Sunset. But *that* will be a totally different Company!

I'll just go and see if breakfast is ready . . .

D'you mind closing the window . . .?

The author as a boy.

THE HOLE IN THE HEDGE

It was Grandma and Grandpa and their four unmarried daughters, who took me over from my foster-parents when the time came, and brought me up. The eldest, — Minnie, — became the Mother-figure.

We lived in a fairly large country house, with a fairly large garden. But then *everything* was large, and the grown-ups were all giants — if you can remember back that far.

But it was in the country, and secluded. A lane ran up through the fields to the house. Beyond that, it dwindled into a footpath.

Aunt Minnie did not mind if I played in the lane — provided I did not wander too far. But I remember Grandma saying, "I don't *like* that lane! There's something funny about it. It gives me a queer feeling."

Aunt Minnie did not take much notice of this. But I did. Because it gave *me* a queer feeling, too. It was as if *someone,* — not unlike my foster-Mother, — was waiting for me. Just round the corner.

The world has very definite limits when you are young. Outside the garden I had extended mine from the back garden gate, and on up to that corner. And then one day, I peeped round.

There was nobody there . . .

It was like Fairyland. Another short stretch lay before me. There was an avenue of tall tree-trunks. The verges were crowded with elm runners, as high as myself.

I remember it lit by a pale, transluscent green from the canopy high overhead. I remember the great coarse folds of hogweed. And the cuckoo-pint hood with its purple thumb standing secretive, inside.

I entered cautiously into this green silence. Then I felt that someone — *was* there. It was a woman. I looked round for her. But I could not see anything.

A little way along, I found a twisted, narrow path. It led-off between tall weeds to a hole in the hedge; and the sun shone bright behind it.

That woman. Perhaps she was on the other side of the hedge . . .?

It was only a little path, and I crept along, and looked through the hole. There was nobody there again . . .

But the *world* was there! I did not know it was so huge. It went on and on for ever before me . . .

I did not venture into it — it was much too large. I just stayed near the field verge, and played in the sun.

It was not until I re-entered the lane, that I heard Aunt Minnie's voice. She stood between the hedges in her long dress. And she was very cross.

"Where have you *been?*"

"In the field, Auntie."

"Why didn't you answer when I called?"

"I didn't hear you."

She grabbed me by the hand, and I almost had to run to keep up with her.

However, I was allowed later on to play up there again. I had been told that when Auntie called, I was to answer *at once*. Otherwise I would *not* be allowed — out of the garden!

The new stretch of lane was now added to my world — and I gradually became accustomed to the expanse of the real world on the other side of the hole in the hedge.

I don't know when I realised there was a house there. I can remember quite a bit of what it looked like. It was long, with a low, thatched roof, and tall white chimney-pots.

Beside the open door, on a bench by the wall, sat a lady. I remember *her* very well. Her hair was done up in a bun on the top of her head. She wore a long, long dress, and a big white apron. Her sleeves were rolled up, and she had a bowl on her lap, peeling potatoes. Further to the left, a donkey was browsing. And at the far end of the house, I saw a donkey-cart.

I remember there nothing strange to me about it. It was all completely familiar. As familiar in fact as my early impressions of my own home. The woman who sat there gave me the same feelings of safety, completeness, as did Aunt Minnie.

I cannot account for this. Except, perhaps, by the well-known fact that in the mind of the very young child, there is little division between dream, fancy, reality. But the odd thing was, that when I was there, if Auntie called me, her voice came down to me from out of the sky. And when I answered, *my* voice went up into the sky as well.

The dream-picture — if dream-picture it was, — began to fill-in. There was a man in it, as well as a lady. He was about at odd times. I remember how he would disappear into a wooden outhouse. And to the accompaniment of a great deal of noise of chopping, I could see him, just in the door, working there. And every so often, he would come out with a bundle of pea-sticks which he stacked by the wall of the house. When he had made enough bundles, he would harness the donkey to the cart, load up the peasticks, and lead the animal off towards the sandpits.

I remember it all very well. The load jogging off down the rough road. The jacketed and gaitered figure at the donkey's head. The tread of heavy boots, the rattle of iron-tyred wheels. The light clip-clop of the donkey.

Sometimes the man was there all the time — digging, in his garden. And I would stand on the garden path, watching the worms swirl out to the surface, as he dug along the rows.

He was always at work. I remember the strength of his hands, his crooked, stubby fingers; the corns on his palms, and the deep, deep lines on his face.

Both woman and man were usually much too busy to take much notice of me. But at the same time, they were not *strangers.*

Then came another incident. One day, the woman came out and said, "Dinner-time, son." I knew exactly what to do . . .

From the butt in the corner between porch and cottage, she dipped out rainwater with a hand bowl. She placed it on a bench. As I stood there, washing my hands and playing with the soap, the man came up behind me. He put both arms round me — and I knew we had played this game many times before. I squeezed the soap, it shot up, and he caught it. We both laughed.

Then we went in to dinner. It was a small room, with clean sacks on the flags, an open fireplace. There was no tablecloth. Enamel plates were set upon a scrubbed deal table. I had my own little two-pronged fork with a yellow bone handle, and a small knife with a black wooden one. I had a wooden spoon.

I sat on one side of the table; the man sat in a wooden armchair on the other side to my right, the woman to the left. The meal served, I put my hands together, and closed my eyes for Grace.

When I did this, I heard Auntie's voice outside, insistent, urgent. "Wake up! Wake up, boy!''

Startled, I opened my eyes. She was bending over me. She was very cross because 'I had given her a turn' as she said. And if I wanted to sleep, I was to come indoors, and not curl up under the hedge where I could not be seen.

I was again grabbed by the hand, and almost run home. So I had little chance to tell her she was wrong about me sleeping under the hedge, or where I had really been. Could I have done so, I think this final, appalling episode might never have been allowed to happen.

For punishment, this time I *was* confined to the garden. But one day, Aunt Minnie got on her bicycle, and cycled off down the lane to visit a friend in Romsey.

Grandma and Grandpa were having their afternoon nap indoors. The rest of my Aunts were away at their work. So I was lonely, and bored. And wandered back into the lane . . .

I went back through the hole in the hedge, and played and played in the garden, and the sun shone, and the day went by. I heard no-one calling. But I do remember a lapwing up in the sky, crying, and crying. Anxiously — so that I noticed it.

I asked the man in the garden why she was crying. He said, "Somebody is too close to her little ones. She's afraid they'll be took away."

The man left digging after a while. I followed him on down to the cottage. He went into his little outhouse. I stood in the doorway, looking into the gloom. He was working at a bench at the far end, by the light filtering through a cobwebby window. Then I saw what he was doing. He was making a wooden doll. The limbs were of shaped wooden beads, articulated by string threaded through them. Deftly, he cut out eyes, ears, nostrils, mouth, in the largest bead for the head. Then he put it together, painted it, black, red and white, and put it out on the tin roof of the building in the sun, to dry. He said, "That's for a good boy! But wait until the paint's dry."

I could hardly contain my impatience through the day. But at last, after tea, when it was becoming dusk, he came into the living room with it. And I took it, while I sat, in my long night-gown, on the woman's lap before the fire.

Candlestick in hand, the woman later preceded me up the steep creaking stairs. We went into a little bedroom with a sloping ceiling. I was put into a large cot with iron rails in a sort of whorl-pattern, all around it.

Again it was nothing strange. I knew the bedroom well, and all that it contained. I sat up in bed, put my hands together, and said my prayers. I arranged my wooden doll, its head on the pillow beside mine. The woman bent down and kissed me, then tip-toed out. A dim light filtered in through the dormer window.

I heard the lapwing still crying. Crying and crying, until I fell asleep . . .

Next day, I was out playing in the garden again, and the sun shone. As usual, the woman came out later on to sit on her bench by the cottage door, and prepare the midday meal. She said;

"Don't go out of the garden, will you?" I said that I would not.

And then, when I was again near the hole in the hedge, I was startled to hear Aunt Minnie's voice, calling from the other side.

I heard more than this. I heard the sound of men breaking through the undergrowth; dogs being whistled. And one, a huge lop-eared animal, burst through farther along by the garden, and came bounding towards me.

The woman jumped to her feet, scattering the bowl and all its contents to the ground. She came running up the garden path, and I remember how she looked; for because of her long dress, she seemed to be gliding without moving her legs.

I remember her face — vividly. It had changed. She was wide-eyed. Her hair had slipped into disarray, and her hands were stretched out towards me. She was a wild, alarming figure. The great dog had seen her, and sped towards her, its teeth bared.

I fled in terror. My legs would not seem to move fast enough — the tiny path seemed endless long. I heard behind me the throaty snarls of the dog, the wild screaming of the woman. I stumbled — straight into Auntie's arms. She held me close, and I remember the trees above our heads bowed suddenly in a rush of wind . . .

Of course there was great upheaval and questioning and tears and goodness knows what. I don't recollect too clearly, but I did manage to tell my Grandparents and my Aunts about the house, the man and the woman, and the bedroom where I had slept. I still clutched the wooden doll. I remember Grandpa saying, "I'll find out who held him if its the last thing I do!" But they never did find out . . .

Well — I am married and middle-aged now, with children of my own. My relatives have died — but up to a short time ago, I still had the wooden doll. For some reason or other, I was always disinclined to let my children touch it. So it hung on a nail on the inside wall of the woodshed.

A week or so ago I was in there, when an old traveller appeared in the doorway, asking for rags and old iron. I said I did not think we had any.

He was just about to go, when he caught sight of the wooden doll. He said, "Where did you get that?" I said I found it, when I was a little boy.

The gypsy was very interested. He wanted to know where I had found it. I told him the village, the lane, the field.

He pressed me further — so I told him about my dream. He believed me.

He said: "Guv'nor — you should not keep that thing on the place wi' young children about! Thank God you never let 'em touch it! They ha' gone you know! They'd ha' gone — same as you did when you was a boy!"

Then he told me that years ago, — somewhen in the 1840's, — there *had been* a cottage where I had seen my dream-house and a couple living there, and one boy. The man was a spar and hurdle and wooden toy maker. "And," said the gypsy, "My old folks often used to talk about 'em because they knew 'em. They comed from our own people, and he made wooden toys for to sell. They built the house with chalk walls theirselves — and then arter it all happened, the two on 'em jes walked out and left it — and went back to the roads. The house fell apart, and the chalk walls was carted and spread on the land by the farmers. The other bits went, bit by bit."

I asked, "What *did* happen then?"

He said, "That little boy o' their'n — they never 'lowed out o' the garden. But one day he got through a hole in the heidge. When they come to look far'n he couldn't be found. And he never *was* found Guv'nor — livin' nor deid. I wouldn't 'ave that thing about if I was you!"

I took it off the nail and offered it to him. He waved it away. It was consigned to the very next bonfire . . .

Never again found, living or dead. If I could only remember where I *really* found that wooden doll — I wonder if the mystery of that old village tragedy might yet be solved?

OCTOBER MORNING 1976
Binley and St. Mary Bourne

We are nearly at the end of British Summer Time. Dawn is some-where around seven o' clock. Not too great a hardship, therefore, (not forgetting mackintoshes and Wellington boots,) to motor up to the hills around Binley, between Whitchurch and St Marybourne, to see the sunrise.

As we enter Binley, headlights pick-up the pub. They flare between the banks of the narrow lane. Walls of farm cottages on our right stand like momentary photographic images, then flick-flick-flick behind. Then there's the big farmhouse on the left, the dark shape of the milking-bale on our right and — steady — we turn in here.

It's a bit bumpy along this track. It only leads to a field . . .

There's the five-barred gate at the end . Switch-off. Switch out the lights. Yes it is rather dark. Our eyes will get used to it in a minute . . .

No need to lock-up here. Watch-out for hanging brambles and twigs — you can easily get one in your eye. Let's lean over the gate until the light comes up . . .

There you are — the long, black line of the North Hampshire Downs. That cloud sitting above them — it's like a huge, black hand lying there, palm upwards. Sunlight begins to glow behind the thumb. It travels up behind it like a hidden flare — and — here it comes — the sun! Bursting upon us in a blaze, and a vague warmth deflected to us already from that inky canopy of cloud.

Mists stirr from their long night's sleep. They gather gently together, and pour like huge rivers up the valleys towards us. Incredibly long shadows lying across hilltop fields. Cowpaths winding away down to the farmstead like crooked ravines. Pasture coated with dew-dust, light blue. Hoarse voices of rooks sailing one behind the other over the hazels, then swooping low to the ground on the other side. Sometimes giving a bronchial chuckle.

Jays rasp.

The mists now reach us, creeping-out from copse and laneside hedge, cloying and cold. So we are enveloped in dark again — momentarily.

Screech-owls re-awaken and begin to call each other. Sparrows seem alarmed. The robin ticks nervously. Can you hear — far away towards St Mary Bourne, — the geese giving their morning greeting to their owner?

Wreathes and swirls of mist. Endlessly passing. Light waxing and waning — and all of a sudden, the mists gone. Except for those few straggling wraiths which miraculously vanish as they come, before they can catch the grey hosts hurrying-on towards St. Mary Bourne.

Down in the mudyard beside the milking-bale, dim shapes of cows. Easing patiently from hoof to hoof. Boss cows pressing the still closed half-doors; all standing in order of seniority, grading back to the restless and nervous and timid at the rear.

Sometimes there is a stir like a breeze among them. Black legs then make moving triangles before steel mirrors of pools and filled-in hoof castes. Dehorned head push and swing irritably — until seniority is established again.

Lights go up in the milking bail. Boss cows are alerted. The white smudge of a human face surveys them as the top half of the doors swings open. A voice travels up to us,

"They bain't all yere!"

How well I know *that* routine! How well I know the answer!

"Bain't all yere?"

"No — they bain't! Old Molly ain't yere!"

"You sure?"

"Can't see 'er! Cans't thee?"

"No — buggered if I can! And I hucked 'er out thee's knaw!"

"Ha — she must ha' doubled-back on thee in the dark!"

"Sod it, then!"

Here comes the man who said 'Sod it!' out of the shadows. Stumping along, head down with annoyance — and off up one of the cowpaths. Past a row of concrete blocks he goes, still guarding the entrance to Binley from a German tank-invasion that never came. And you can see now tall sorrel-stems standing in a rank like soldiers, behind them.

Past the cock-ended trailer with the unmistakable minute bobbing of the robin on its point. Past the pyramid of maple-leaves, with red-and-brown seeds glowing like bunches of jewels in washed sunlight. And up over the skyline towards the sleeping skeletons of larch.

The boss cow has been milked. She emerges leisurely from the bail's other side. She has eaten her ration of dry bait which brought her in to be milked, and immediately makes for the water-trough. Gently, she thrusts her head forward to the water; lips touching the surface, nostrils well above, with the utmost delicacy.

Another emerges; approaches diffidently, and does the same at the far end. The boss cow lifts her head, drips gleaming as they fall from her chin. The other rolls an eye towards her. The boss carries on drinking — all is well.

Another emerges, and yet another. These two approach the trough, and stand waiting a little way from it. The boss moves off slowly to wait at the outlet gate, and the others move-in to drink.

Colour emerges as the light strengthens, in the track behind us. Long knitting needles of spindle show orange beads in pink velvet boxes, and yellow-green leaves which seem to have been dipped in red ink. There are mottled blacks and browns and reds of wayfaring trees; tall ranks of purple-stemmed dogwood. There are necklaces of giant berries, waxed and red, strewn over the hedges. Water-colour elders, scarlet wild-rose urns. Privett berries, bulbous blue, and tall, dry skeletons of hogweed.

There are brown bunches of sycamore seed. Conkers fall, and hazel leaves have turned from yellow and gold to dried and lifeless brown, as have the leaves of stub-oak.

Hallo — here's Molly! Lumbering the brow of the hill; nostrils wide, eyeball and neck at strain, shoulders heaving, back arched against the force of inadequate haunches trying to propel the udder-flying, tail-flailing bulk of a creature built for slow and heavy grace, at unaccustomed speed. The furious returning human figure also at unaccustomed speed, so that his stumping legs and elbows jerk at each labouring breath, turning him into a black and malevolent spider as he, too, appears over the brow.

But he knows — and Molly knows — the head man will have none of this. Turn a cow in all of a 'hu-ha' and she won't give down her milk.

So Molly slows-down as soon as she sees the milking-bale. The figure behind bottles his rage, and slows too. The tables are turned. Out of sight of the head man, Molly was the helpless victim. But now she is in confident, — even contemptous, — control of her boiling oppressor behind.

84

A vale-sheltered oak-group, leaves not yet turned, together catch the sunlight. They perform the curious illusion of together turning into piles and pyramids of green glass marbles.

A slanting drift of white smoke behind them, followed by the sound of a starting tractor. While stockman near the end of their first stint, and look forward to their breakfasts, landsmen have had theirs and begin their day.

The tractor comes out from behind the oaks, trailer piled high with manure from the hen batteries, and makes for the arable. Arriving, the driver dismounts. He goes to the trailer rear, loosens the backboard fixtures. He remounts, and as he goes on, the trailer slowly tips, to spread this dry, hot, gassy fertiliser along the soil.

It can be ploughed-in immediately; so next to come is the ploughman, cocked mouldboards winking behind him, bumping his way to the edge of the furrows.

Settled, the plough drops. The ploughman checks 'arter and avore'. All well, a black-and-brown burst fires from his exhaust, tails off white, and then disappears as away he goes.

Now you can see the flocks travelling towards him across the valley. On purposeful, deliberate flight-lines — the round-winged, softly-moving plovers. They carpet the ploughland, restlessly active before sorting themselves out.

Now settled against the dark arable — they have almost disappeared. If we hadn't seen them come — we wouldn't know they were there. Except — look! — for the odd glint of Japan green, as one bird or another turns its body against the sun. Or that flash of white as one raises its wings to balance.

We must wait . . .

Now you can see how they begin to work the ground, all moving the same way, each leaving a clear working-space for the other. In that way, the whole field is minutely quartered.

Those at the edge of the flock take-on sentry duty. They watch as much as they feed. Their job is to warn of danger, to lead flight should it approach too close.

The field quartered, they might break up into separate smaller flocks to other feeding-grounds during the day. This time of year, although they do arrive and depart on the same flight-line, they might still be in their separate flocks. It is when the immigrants come in from the Continent in a week or two's time, that they all conjoin to form the huge concourses of winter. And stay in them until the time of departure, seperation, courtship and breeding comes again.

They are hauling bales to the fattening-sheds. Both driver and his mate on the trailer are masked. At least here the Ministry's drive against 'Farmer's Lung' — due to mould-spores from bales and stored grain, — is being acted upon.

The country 'idyll' is not what it was. Scientific research, implements and methods alter almost everything year by year. Even the hurdlemaker exchanges his treasured hook, blacksmith-made for his grandfather from a worn-out rasp for trimming the hooves of the great Shires, for the mechanical saw when he cuts down the wands from the hazel-stools. His market now, since the advent of sheep-control by sheep-wire instead of hurdles, is fencing for the home and garden.

The pigman comes out to scatter rations to his dry sows in their concrete yards. They have never felt grass or earth beneath their feet from birth, and nor will their offspring until death. They say the cost of treating earth and vegetation-borne diseases, outstrips that of supplying vitamins and drugs, to offset the infections and tensions of artificially crowded 'factory farming' conditions. All right economically I suppose. But I wonder how much of these drugs we build-up in ourselves, from eating the pork and bacon?

I remember old Charlie Vane looking over his sty at his cottage pigs elbow-deep in mire. He said,

"They dun't 'urt! They thrives on it! I'd sooner eat they than what you gets in the shops!

"Bacon?" he said. "Wi' the pig *still alive* only a week or fartnight afore? Tain't possible!"

Grey clouds with soft ragged edges hurry-in over the trees. The wind rises. Listen — a multitude of whispers in the kale, — rain pattering-in like a greeting.

Maples turn their backs to it all. The thorn-tree down on the field corner waves black ostrich feathers. And here it comes — rain! Knocking down showers of water-colour-mauve leaves from the elder tree, spinning plates from the walnut, stained black.

Rooks swirl-up with the autumn leaves, like black fragments of humus stirred in a stagnant pool. The farm buildings, trailerman and ploughman vanish in a grey rain-sheet. The herd turns like weather-vanes backs towards the storm. Water rushes from the ditch beside the bail, and spreads across the concrete. The next to be milked blunders in, rain spouting from her coat in rivulets — did you hear the cowman's roar, "Fer Christ's seake — STEADY gal!"

All right — back in the car — and home for breakfast . . .

It was only a shower . . .

If you can glance to the right — that's the Bourne look, nearly empty again. It stays dry all the winter. It flows again round about January, and disappears around October. In a normal year, that is. There are several bournes like this in the East of Hampshire. There's Finchley, and King's Somborne as well, which we'll soon be passing through.

A Water-Board man told me they stay dry all the winter because they are fed from the chalk-hills. When it rains, there is no flow overland on chalk to feed the springs; the water soaks straight through. It's when the chalk-hills get saturated that the water comes out of them and the bournes begin to flow. By October, the hills are generally dry again, so the bournes are empty.

So there you are. Plenty to see in the countryside, even in October. No need to stay cooped-up in the town or indoors . . .

Look at that chap's onions — they're late! But they're not bad, are they . . .?

And there's the old water-keeper by his eel-traps, picking-up the last of the run . . .

Opposite: The pigman comes out to scatter rations to his dry sows in their concrete yards.   *(Photograph: W. H. Rendell)*

Wasn't it Strange?

I remember — sitting on Len's shoulder. He was my foster-brother.

It was down in the orchard at West's Cottages, Baughurst. Foster-Father Frank West, was pushing-up the bonfire with an ash-handled prong. There were some little girls, side-by-side, in front of a row of beehives, all white. I remember they had long dresses on, down over their knees. The big boys were over on the other side, in the dark.

Guy-Fawkes flared up, and he had a face made of cardboard. All of a sudden his face folded up — and it was gone!

A long time ago. I couldn't have been older than — three . . .

I remember the ship. It was after I'd left my foster-parents, and my own people had taken me on. Grandad had retired from Mottisfont; he was a station-master. They took up the line some years ago.

Grandma was there, and Aunt Tory on leave from Africa — she was a Headmistress in a Johannesburgh school for girls. Aunt Minnie was there, who stayed home to help Grandma. So was Aunt Ethel, who taught the infants down at Romsey Abbey. And so was Aunt Nora, who taught at Regents Park Southampton, and Aunt Vera, who was a booking-clerk on the old Southern Railway. And Ida, my Mother, who was on the telephones at Salisbury Station with Uncle Frank, who was a porter.

My future step-Father, Arthur Gibson, a Southern Railway depot Superintendent down at Southampton Docks, he, too was there. I called him 'Uncle Arthur'. He took charge of the fireworks in the backyard, because the women were nervous about lighting the fuses.

The *ship*. It was set-up on a bank on the other side of the yard. There was a label on it — AQUITANIA. All lights were put out — the ship was the climatic piece to our family firework display.

It was lovely. Beautiful blue smoke billowed out of its funnels. It rolled away through the fence, and into the darkness of the field beyond. There were rows of cabin windows, all lit up. And two white masts, with paper Union Jacks stuck on their tops.

Then — the ship went BANG! — and had gone! The women all shouted together "OH!" And Uncle Arthur laughed. And I laughed because *he* laughed; and because they all shouted "OH!" Otherwise — I would have been frightened to death.

I went to look for the pieces in the morning. I *wanted* that ship . . .

A piece of singed card, folded. A few burned-out stubs. Nothing else there . . .

That's all I remember of that. And *that* was a long time ago . . .

It's a long time, too, since from my window, which faces the village green, I saw the last of a once familiar Bonfire Night routine.

Hoards of children used to come out from the copse, dragging any fallen wood they could find. Parents got rid of loads of rubbish. By November 5th, there would be a bonfire blocking the view. With a giant Guy on the top, dressed in clothes we recognised. Because we'd seen them walking about in the village, before they were claimed for sacrifice.

The *last* time it happened, there weren't hoards. There were just two. A little boy and a little girl, — with the little girl very much in charge. Dragging away on a branch much too large for them.

I went out to give a hand. Like me, Willie from next door was an avid collector of bits which might come in handy. So we both had a turn-out.

Others along the road did the same. When the sparse little crowd of remaining village children came down in the evening after school, (already due for closure,) they bore a Guy. So it was still a quite respectable bonfire after all.

On the night, our two older sons, — once well in the lead with bonfire preparations, — went off somewhere with friends. The two daughters were stuck in front of the Telly. Only the youngest lad, and the then three-year-old baby girl were excited.

The lad went off out in the darkness to meet-up with others. I took the baby in my arms up to the front bedroom window, and pulled-back the curtains . . .

Children's voices in the fields blackness. Footfalls on the road; but not the clatter and scuffle of tipnailed boots of days gone by. The anxious warning from Willie next door —

"You stay 'ere wi' *me,* Peter! John — don't you go lightin' that there thing in your 'and!''

A match flared. A flame leaped — then went out. This happened two or three times. Then — a sudden rush of flame as Willie tipped-in some paraffin . . .

The bonfire got under way, casting its ring of light. Like animated dwarfs, the children drew-in from the strange things of the night standing outside the edge of the light-circle. A few poised adult faces. Disembodied by darkness . . .

And then, rooted in the grass with toes white with light, I *did* see a pair of tipnailed boots. I looked harder at the dim figure.

Sure enough, there once again was my old colleague from the days when I was a farm worker. Pipe-in-mouth, cap pulled down over one eye, every year Old Stan tramped down from his cottage on the hill. He would never miss a Bonfire Night.

I wonder why . . .?

I remember after one sowing-time on the farm, we were left with a pile of empty paper fertilizer-bags. I said to Stan,

"What are we going to do with them?''

"Burn 'em!'' he said. "Burn 'em!''

We put them in a heap and set fire to them. He watched. There was a curious fascination in his eyes. Suddenly, he ran forward, — pulled out a burning bag, waved it around so that the sparks flew from it in a red cloud, and spun it in the air. He did it again . . . and again. He danced, clumsily; *shouted,* red-faced and excited. And then seemed — almost embarrassed at what he had done.

I don't think anybody — except children — would do anything like that, these days . . .

Wasn't it *strange . . .?*

NOVEMBER MORNING, 1950
Heron Lane, Timsbury.

It was not so very cold for the time of year. The fog, a luminous grey, was in close attendance. I guided myself by following the damp, bedraggled hedge, which I knew would lead out into the lane.

Moisture sogged in the verge grass beneath my feet. When I stood still, I could hear a strange, magnetic song. It was like the all-prevading hiss you sometimes hear, just before you go to sleep. It came from the very dampness of the hedges — from the thickset of the hawthorn, the tangled bramble-hill. It was in the rose-bush with its wet-stained, thorn-silhouetted arms. It came from the matted heads of Old Man's Beard, from verge-growth, couch, dogwood, sodden-barked elder. It came from the matt of leaf-fall, and above all, from the circle of the fog itself.

Perhaps that all-prevading sound, and the shortened visibility, accounted for my surprising half a dozen blackbirds, busy among the remaining haws. Too startled to speak, they fluttered on a yard or so ahead. They paused in a bunch on a clearer take-off point. Fixed upon me was a battery of scandalised, yellow-rimmed black lenses. Then the fog-dome enclosing us magnified their clattering alarm, and they vanished in the wake of their leader, ahead.

A robin trilled its annoyance at the bubbub. I looked for his little image. I could just see his red signal deep in the tangle — but he was not particularly put-out.

A bottle-tit lingered, its colours blending with the browns and yellows and greens. A wren shot silently from the underwood, to whir on its way in tiny loops and dips low to the ground, in the wake of the blackbirds.

Mixed company at the feast. But it was not all avian life . . .

A half-eaten haw low down in the hedge with yellow flesh still bright, made me search among leaf-fall on the grey soil beneath. Sure enough I found a few haw-stones, scattered by the vole.

On many of the berries themselves, there was a pin-prick hole in the skin, surrounded by a minute area of bruised flesh. The same type of bruising you might see around the area where a wasp has been at an apple.

Too late in the year now to search for the visitor. But up until a short time ago it, bright green-and-red in the sun, — a little bug, piercing and sucking.

I saw other creepy-crawlies, long-antennaed and spotty-legged, descending with merciless pincers upon soft-bodied, grey-green aphids, and eating them alive.

Turning one single leaf less than an inch square, I saw all this as well. A large aphid, say a millimetre and a half long, semi-transparent, wavering as if panic-stricken from side to side. Beside it, half a dozen or so minute versions of itself, in a circular bunch. The circle shrank as they rushed in together, then expanded as they rushed apart. Then, too far apart for the comfort and security of each others' company, the circle again shrank as they rushed together once more, and stayed still.

A reaction I supposed, to being suddenly turned from their shaded world into bright daylight. I wondered if the large one was the parent? It could have been. Naturalists tell us how some of these minute creatures have a surprisingly protective instinct for their young.

Where did they come from? Perhaps from under that little flat cacoon. But underneath *that* was another creature; a tiny caterpillar already hatched

A wren in the undergrowth. (Photograph: James Carr)

— and I supposed, waiting for the spring.

But — a conundrum. I could understand the glistening wee white eggs of the hairstreak butterfly stuck on the twigs, waiting through the winter to hatch-out as caterpillars for next year's leaf-budding. But this community on the back of a leaf which was going to *fall* — what would happen to *them* through the winter?

Anyway, they and their like, and tiny things like butterfly-eggs rather than berries, accounted for the presence of the blue-tit and the wren at the feast, with the robin a casual dabbler, — because he'll eat anything from spiders to berries.

On — and the rich, shiny, half-rooted red of overripe rose-hips.

I picked-out one or two hips smaller than the others. Sure enough, on the side of each, a single small hole choked with minute debris. Each empty of the yellow-bright, silver-downed seed.

If you open these earlier in the year, the cause is evident. Its's a caterpillar which eventually emerges via the hole provided by its thoughtful parent, and turns into the night-moth.

I thought the rose-hip crop looked a bit denuded already. It was not due to birds. As yet, we had had no fieldfare or redwing weather. And their cousins, the thrushes and blackbirds only seem to go for them as a last resort.

The squirrel and the tree-rat will have a go — but briefly. But here, hip-stalks had been systematically cut-off, and there was a scatter of minute red-and-yellow debris, — again quite fresh, — directly beneath on the frost-darkened leaves.

Long lines of freshly-ploughed land nearby, would be the reason why. Fieldmice had come in temporarily to the hedgerows, while Armaggedon descended upon their patiently and logically-built world of runs and tunnels, because of the plough.

I have seen them climb to the topmost berries, nip them off at the stalks, and then sit there tackling them like tiny squirrels. Holding the berry in their paws, while they stripped the flesh with little chisel teeth, to reach the seeds inside.

Dangerous this — so exposed! But those bulging, glistening black eyes can see above, below, behind, before, — all at the same time! The little animal reacts to every countryside movement. Never still for more than a fraction of a second.

So any enemy must be *at once* — on target! Miss — and it skips aside — and is gone!

I saw hazel-nut shells with neat, circular holes in them. This is the field-mouse's work too — or the vole's. The squirrel and tree-rat, — like the rest of us, — *cracks* the shell into fragments, to get at the nut inside.

But after the hubbub in the fields ceases with the departure of plough, cultivator, drill and harrow, field-mouse and vole will be back in the fields again to take their chances with weasel, stoat, snake if the late-to-bed female adder is still about; or with gull, kestrel, owl, crow, rook. But maybe the rook will be merciful; replete as he must now be with wireworm and leatherjacket, turned-up across Hampshire's winter acres by the ton, which will next year transform themselves into beetles, and Daddy-long-Legs.

Many soil beetles, being carniverous, do us a power of good among soil pests. What the Daddy-long-Legs does, I am not quite sure. Except to charm us by its soft, transparent-winged delicate flight, which it somehow sustains in quite strong winds, and its long, gentle, slender legs.

Last month I saw a Daddy — or Mother! — long Legs, urgently searching the garden clods; tail down, as if weakened and fallen. Not at all. She was searching for some root into which to lay her eggs!

Bad luck for me in the Spring, especially if as a result of this I get leatherjackets in my seed potatoes! But I let her get on with it. I think she dies after she has laid her eggs — but I am not sure . . .

Spindle; that beautiful shrub, this time of year with slender leaf-points seemingly dipped in ink, red and mauve. Yellow seeds peeping from purple, three-corner-folds, — the greatest miscreant of all! There is a giant specimen in the corner of my garden. I ought to know better, really, but it has thrived there, undisturbed, for fifty years. Haunted by tits and other small birds in winter, looking for the eggs of aphids, — black aphids.

If you plant your broad beans too late, — it is best to sow them in November or early October, — they will certainly catch the 'fly'. There used to be a lot of superstition in the countryside about the 'fly'. 'Thunder-flies' the old folk called them and thought, because they appeared when the weather was 'lowerin'' and heavy, that they came from the inky-black thunderclouds. A sort of curse or murrain from the Almighty — when he was in one of his nastiest moods!

'The vly, the vly, the vly be on the tarmut!' And it will infest and ruin the carrots, onions, the runners and broad beans too!

But of course, we know better these days. These sap-sucking aphids overwinter, each on their own separate species of plant; and the spindle is host to the bean blackfly.

About April or May the eggs hatch. The tiny creatures are then wingless, and might breed several generations before they produce those with wings which, maybe by some chemistry in the air just before storm, will let them take flight and be carried, quite at random, — a pestilent cloud on the prestorm wind. If they land on your beans, they are lucky — and you aren't! If they don't — they just die.

So down at the pub you might hear a countryman say,

"I got the jugger'n vly!" And his neighbour will say, not perhaps without a smirk of satisfaction,

"'Ave ye? Well I'm blowed! *Mine's* all right — I ain't got narn a speck!''

November 1983.

So from the hedgerows and the copses come plague and pest; part of the reason why they are cleared — to the detriment of the appearance of our countryside. But the trouble is that farm and orchard crops are developed from related wild species. Cereals are grasses. Carrots are the relations of hogweed, Queen Anne's Lace, hemlock. Apple, pear, plum, hawthorn, blackthorn, bullace, rose — are all in some way related.

When we farm, then, we produce a huge artificial ideal environ for aphids and rusts and fungi, which normally would circulate on the wild relations of our crops. And be kept in check by birds and mammals and insects as I have described. The process so aptly summed-up in the old doggerel:

'Big fleas have smaller fleas upon their backs to bite 'em — And smaller fleas have lesser fleas — and so ad infinitum!''

So we have a countryside empting of tree and shrub, which until the rise and effectiveness of the conservationists, was encouraged both advisedly and financially by the agricultural experts in Government who had found all this out. As they do with the huge yearly programme of poison sprays.

No use to talk about 'Upsetting the Balance of Nature'. Farmers always did do that, and had always to find their own ways of making an artificial balance.

But, apart from the fact that today's farming slowly creates a countryside consisting merely of houses, surrounding gardens, (if you are lucky!), earth and roads, — leading to nowhere in particular except to more isolated houses, earth and roads, modern farming as we well know, does not always succeed in creating that artificial balance.

Perhaps somewhere along the line that accounts for such tragedies as the devastation of our elms. For the further threatened devastation by disease of our beeches, our oaks, and other trees which have been our familiar habitat for centuries.

Perhaps that is why in handling some of our crops these days, to avoid lung damage from fungus spores we must use masks?

Perhaps so, perhaps not. But I think it is true to say that very often such vistations can be traced eventually — back to Man himself.

Do you remember the book which came out years ago called 'Silent Spring'? Do you remember how they scoffed, the scientific and the politicians at the authoress Rachel Carson? How they chuckled and categorised her with the 'Doom-watchers' as those who warn are now laughingly called?

Next Spring, go and stand in the middle of one of our modern prairielands, getting larger and larger about us. Look, — and above all, *listen,* — for yourself.

If you have any idea of the teeming, noisy life, the incredible variety, and the kaleidoscope of colour that our countryside once was, when you come back — you won't be chuckling . . .

THE CHRISTMAS TREE

The night before Christmas Eve, Charlie Roach the Keeper stood in the dark passageway behind the bar of the Malt House Inn. The Landlord passed him on his way up from the cellar. He said in a low voice,

"'Allo Charlie! Bitter?"

Charlie nodded. The Landlord drew it, passed it to him. Charlie paid, without coming into full view of the bar . . .

The Landlord went up behind his bar, looked round. Nobody wanted anything. He came back.

"'Ow's things wi' you then, Charlie? Any trouble?"

"Not lately. I lost a few. Close to Christmas now — should be all right. Everybody's got whatever they've got. There's always old Amos o' course. Is 'e about?"

"'E's in there!"

Charlie relaxed. His beer tasted better, knowing where Amos was. He listened. He was used to listening . . .

"I s'pose they cockbirds o' yourn is gone, Amos?"

"Ah! I done-in the last one yest'day!"

"That'll be yourn, then?"

"No!"

"Ha!" said another voice. "Cain't see old Amos sett'n down to a *cockbird* for Christmas! 'E'll 'ave summat better'n that!"

"Matter o' fact," said Amos, "I ain't got nothen in the 'ouse at all!"

"Noth'n?"

"Noth'n!"

"Cawd — an' you sett'n yere wi' per best cwoat on?"

"'E wun't 'ave 'e on b' marnen, I'll be bound!" said another voice.

"Course I shain't! I'll be gwine to work — same as you!"

"Oh ah! Where at?"

"Trimmin' back afore the plough. Up alonzid L-field . . ."

Amos Penfold. A widower. A wiry, cloth-capped, jacketed-and-gaitered man in his late forties. One of the slipperiest poachers Charlie had ever known on his patch. But not a regular — which made him that much more difficult to catch. He usually went poaching when he ran out of casual work. But he could be a nuisance around Christmas time.

Nothing in the house . . .

Charlie thought about that. Might be true. Might be pub-talk.

Working up around L-field . . .

Charlie thought about that, too. Close to where the birds were bred. And still hung about a bit, in spite of the shooting.

H'm . . .

Charlie drank-up, and quietly left . . .

At half past seven, on the morning of Christmas Eve, Charlie Roach stood, — perfectly still, — behind the blackthorn at the edge of L-field. He watched a huge concourse above the trees, the rapidly-glowing light glinting in their wings. The great flock swung lower, and gradually settled among the stubble.

The tractors had only just started-up, down on the farm. Amos would be coming on up before them . . .

He *might* come straight on up Parnel Lane and in at the gap. He might not . . .

He *might* make a try, thinking the coast was clear. If he did, the flock would certainly warn that somebody was about . . .

He might, — like Charlie, — be standing in any one of the tall bushes bordering L-field, watching, waiting, making quite sure . . .

Suddenly, a cock pheasant came out from the hedge alongside Parnel Lane. It paused, raised its long neck, looked carefully round. It stopped, did a bit of pretend-feeding. Then it made for the old rick-stump where they had been threshing.

It dropped its wings stiffly, gave them a partridge-like whirr. It called.

The call was answered from the lane. A number of other birds appeared, and joined it . . .

Then things began to happen . . .

The lapwings, with a great clamour of high-pitched voices, rose from the flock in the field in a huge, flickering, black-and-white swirl. The gulls stayed down but were nervous; a few of the younger ones rose with the lapwings. Only the starlings as if used to all this pother, took not notice of it all.

Gradually, the frightened plovers returned to the stubble. Silent once more — but watchful. Charlie looked across at the pheasants. His practised eye could just distinguish them, now frozen to the earth, like clods.

That was the place to watch! If Amos was going to make his try — it would be *there* . . .*!*

But it was *puzzling,* — that disturbance! It was the kind of demonstration you'd expect when danger — might be more remote . . .

Charlie did not think Amos wold be the cause of *that.* He'd have *seen* the flock settle down into L-field in the first place. He wouldn't have done anything to disturb them — and so give himself away.

The pheasants were on the move again. Scratching like hens in the chaff and the cavings.

Suddenly, the plovers again clamoured, and again rose into the air. The pheasants once more vanished to the ground. It seemed that the whole cycle of events was to be repeated . . .

Then Charlie found himself in the midst of a host of tiny birds. Bluetits, great-tits, long-tailed-tits, chaffinches, linnets, all passing through the blackthorns and bushes about him, with tiny, alarmed cries . . .

But *these* were from the fir-plantation! Amos wouldn't be there! And even if he was — he'd never cause *this* commotion!

Then — it dawned on Charlie! Somebody in the plantation — after the Christmas trees!

All thoughts of Amos gone, Charlie turned and hurried towards this more urgent business! And no sooner had he left his post than there was a furtive movement from behind the rick-stump. A net was cast, and the birds were taken, even as they sat frozen to the ground!

Charlie hurried softly along the drive. As he got nearer to the plantation, he stood still, to listen.

He heard a boy's voice, clear as a bell. He recognised it! If it wasn't young Jim, the image of his father Amos in his walk and ways. Who, like Amos, always crossed to the other side of the road when he saw Charlie, and passed by with his head down and that infuriating, sly grin!

Charlie boiled! Father pinching the birds — and the kids pinching the trees! High time he reckoned, this family was cleared off the Estate! A conviction for pinching Christmas trees would go a long way towards that!

Charlie pressed grimly on. He followed the boundary netting towards the sound. Yes — it was Jim all right — and the whole blooming brood! Young Stanley, Marjorie, and the two five-year-olds, Thurza and John! All gathered round that young devil Jim, who was peeling off his gloves as if he meant business!

Charlie waited. A few cuts into the tree wouldn't hurt — and you had to get evidence!

The older girl said excitedly,

"Bet you cain't do it in one hit, Jim!"

"Don't be daft, Marj! 'Course I cain't! But I'll do it in six! Stand back! Keep they twins out o' the way! Ready?"

"One!" shouted Marjorie and young Stanley together. "TWO! THREE . . .!

The boy missed the next blow and the axe twirled from his grasp and landed in nearby bushes, and they all laughed. He went to retrieve it. And that was when Charlie advanced upon them.

Five pairs of startled eyes turned towards him. Four mouths sagged with fear — but not young Jim's! He left the axe where it lay. *He* was going to blazon it out!

The girl, Marjorie, turned to run away. Jim called sharply,

"Come back there Marj! No need to run away! *We* ain't done nothink!"

The boy faced-up to Charlie.

"We'm only out lookin' for a bit o' firewood, Mr Roach!"

"Firewood, boy? D'you gen'lly chop down green trees for *firewood?"*

The boy put on an air on injured innocence.

"Well — *we* was lookin' at this yere tree — but we never done that! D'you know that, Mister. *We* reckons somebody been up yere tryin' to steal un for Christmas! But *we* never 'ad nothink to do wi' it I'd swear to that anywheres!"

Charlie walked over to the bush where the axe lay, pulled it out and said,

"Well boy — swear to that!"

The boy was still trying.

"That ain't nothink to do w' we, Mister!"

Charlie said, "'Tis no good Jim! I stood there a-watchin' ye! I zid ye cut the tree!"

The boy's courage evaporated, and he stood there wretchedly. There was a little twinge at Charlie's heart. Only a nipper! And a good, hard try . . .

But he said, "Right-ho! Clutter off home the lot on ye! You'd best tell yer Father what's happened. 'E'll *'ave* to know when the P'liceman comes!"

The boy hadn't *quite* given up.

"Can I 'ave my axe, Mister?"

"You *knows* you cain't 'ave your axe, boy. If you took un from your Father wi'out 'is knowin' — they *might* given un back to un — when you have been convicted! And punished!"

The lad led the subdued, miserable little crowd back outside the compound. Charlie watched them go . . .

Somehow, he felt no satisfaction at what he had done. Something was speaking to him — a voice not always the best thing to listen to, for a Keeper! It was a voice called 'Conscience'. It reminded him of the struggle a widower might have being left with all that tribe of children . . . How it might be all the harder if that widower depended on casual work for a living . . . How if they got turned off this Estate, they'd have a job to find anywhere. And them kids *might* end-up in the Workhouse! And all started at Christmas-time! And what would folk think about that . . .?

And the voice said again, that Amos generally only poached when he'd run out of casual work . . . And was only a *nuisance* at Christmas-time . . .

Charlie suddenly said, "Come on back yere! Come on back — the lot of ye . . .!

"Now!" he said as they all trailed back towards him. "You cain't 'ave *this* yere tree 'cause 'e's growed for timber — not for a Christmas tree! 'E's too big. You come along wi' me — and I'll show thee one you *can* 'ave!"

The miserable little faces were transformed with relief and delight.

"Thanks very much Mister!" said the ever-ready Jim.

"I'll thank *thee* very much! You be gwine t' grow-up as cunnin' as a diddicoi — you be! You'm pretty-near 'alf a one, now!"

He led them to the edge of the compound.

"Now then! *This* yer tree's stunted and got a kink in un, 'cause 'e's on the edge o' the copmound and d' catch the wind! You can 'ave '*e* — 'e wun't make good timber! Now you clutter-off down the drive there, Jim, — and you'll find my spade under the lean-to beside my little hut!"

"Be you gwine to dig 'im up, Mister?"

"That's what I'm a-gwine to do. Then you plant 'im in the garden wi' a bit o' sacking round the roots — and use 'im every year! Then you won't 'ave to come up botherin' me no more!"

The boy ran off. Charlie stood there, still trying to look stern. The boy returned with the spade. Charlie handed him the axe and told him he'd no business to have it. Then he dug out the tree, and stood it aside.

"There you are! Now you can see — that's jes the right height!"

They all looked up at it with eyes which had already dressed it with streamers and stars and silver bells and candles and a fairy on the top. Charlie permitted himself a smile.

"Well you cain't carry that axe and the tree as well," he said to Jim, "And 'tis too heavy for young Marj here. I'll bring it down far thee!"

He swung the tree upon his shoulder, and they trailed out of the drive and down the lane behind him.

When Charlie reached Amos's cottage, he was in a jovial mood. But who should be coming up the lane towards him, but the poacher himself?

He looked worried.

"What's on then, Keeper?"

"Mr Roach, he brought us down a Christmas tree — and dug it up hisself!" said Marjorie. "Wasn't that kind of 'im, Dad?"

Amos gave a nervous hitch to his coat.

"You looks as if you'm putt'n on weight, Amos!" observed Charlie. "You'll ha' to' do something about it! Else you won't be able to move fast enough, will 'e?"

Amos didn't answer. It wasn't the time to push his luck . . .

His mood changed, Charlie felt a sudden feeling of warmth towards Amos.

"Look!" he said. "Why don't you clutter-off on to 'Is Lardship's Estate, — and leave my stuff alone? I'll be bound to catch thee sooner or later! I near as dang-it copped thee up in L-field this mornin'!"

And Amos stood there with his coat all loose and heavy around him and said,

"L-field? I ain't been near the place!"

Charlie felt his mood changing again! He threw down the tree and walked away . . .

He knew what Amos had under his coat . . .

He fell to thinking of the conversation in the pub . . .

"Cain't see old Amos sett'n down to a *cockbird* for Christmas . . .!"

And then — that voice that he ought not to listen to if he was going to do a proper job, spoke to him again. And it said,

"*Well,* Charlie Roach! What will *you* be sett'n down to . . .?"

Snow brings hunger to the small birds first, like these Blue and Great Tits pictured on a bird table.   *(Photograph: James Carr)*

DECEMBER MORNING, 1950
Manor Farm, Timsbury.

It's the Dairyman's turn for Christmas with his family. Old Stan and I are relieving him . . .

It's cold. We've only just turned out of bed. So not much is said . . .

We trudge past the Vicarage. The walls throw-back the echo of our boots on the road. Cottages stand, secretive, silent, slates blue with frost. A light shows in a scullery. Tousled shadows move behind drawn curtains. Hover over stoves. And breakfast tables . . .

We cross the style. Frost-crystals are cold and rough to the hands. The tails of our overcoats brush them off the top rail in a shower.

The footpath winds between frosted verges. Through the white field, in a black, twisted line. A Scots Pine towers seasonally into a Christmas-card sky. Magenta spaces, and huge stars floating.

Along the lane, pleaches of thickset, white-robed and rigid, as if they had been stuck group by group into the frost-bound bank.

"Waal!" says Old Stan. "Winter be 'ard! Frost to 'ang white in leane!"

He points to tall elm-skeletons with crowns like huge-canopied, black-twigged hats, huddled on the white hill.

"Trees be all dark. Heidges leary. Snow 'll be back agean!"

We come upon the cows, unwilling to get up from their warm earth-beds; huge black-and-white hulks with a black patch round each, where their body-heat has melted the frost. And curious black rays radiating through the frost from the head of each beast, where their hot breath has shot across the grass and melted it.

Stan worries the boss cow until she eventually lumbers to her feet. Once she's on the move, the others will follow.

But he's gentle with her.

"Dun't 'urry 'em!" he says. "They 'as to step dainty 'cause the ground's like iron. If you 'urries 'em they'll spread their claws and split their feet."

He goes on ahead, calling.

"Cup-cup-come on 'en! Cup-cup-cup-come on!"

A plover calls plaintively from the hill at the disturbance. An owl wheezes fitfully from a dark oak tree. It is answered by the weird call of a vixen. And rooks break into a harsh babble of consternation from the elm tops.

I go round the herd to shift the laggards, then hurry down to catch-up with Stan. We go through the five-barred gate, and close it behind us. The cows collect there, waiting, while we open the cowpen doors and feed round the mangers.

"Frost do 'ang white in leane! Heidges leary. Snow'll be back again!"

The phrases stick in my mind, They *worry* me . . . all day . . .

Stan was right about the snow. In the middle of the afternoon milking, it began to fall down past the half-doors of the cowpen in big flakes. Softening the outlines of the yard fence. Covering the roof-tops so that they blended oddly with a grey-white sky . . .

"Snow d' come back agean!" No — "Snow *will* come back agean!" No — "Snow *d'* come back agean!" is better . . .

I know what is happening . . .

A robin lands on the window-sill outside, mosses thrusting minute, hair-like stems up between its claws. Its red breast is damp, and bedraggled. It puffs-up a little cloud of snow as it suddenly takes-off, flies along the edge of the building and in at the door, and up among the warm rafters above the boiler-house to dry out . . .

The whole world goes silent, and takes on an unreal air. We finish milking, take out a load of bales and break them in the fields . . .

"Christmas be come! Weather be 'ard! Frost to 'ang white in leane! Woods be all dark. Heidges leary. Snaw'd come back agean . . .!"

Yes — that's perfect . . .!

We let the cows out again, close the gate behind them; we can't wash-down but we brush-out as best we can and wash-up in the dairy.

The lights in the village are up as we trudge home. Just as we get to our gate — Old Stan lives next door and we share the front gate, — my two boys come in cold and wet, after a game of snowballing . . .

I can hardly wait to have my tea. Afterwards, I get out my old Oliver typewriter, and I have a go . . .

> Christmas be come!
> Weather be 'ard!
> Frost do 'ang white in leane!
> Woods be all dark.
> Heidges leary.
> Snaw d' come back agean.
>
> Rooks d' bide whoam.
> Plover d' cry.
> Cows be all stood b' geate.
> 'Ouse-mouse d' scratch.
> Dusk d' come down.
> Fleames is all blue, in greate.
>
> Kettle d' zing.
> Tea ben all laid.
> Chillern comes in vrom play.
> Vixen d' scream.
> Owl sets in tree.
> 'Whit-*wheet!* Whit-*wheet!*' he d' zay!

I rush into the kitchen to my wife, full of achievement. But she's busy changing Robin and Adrian in the warm, for bed. And she's got ironing. So I think,

"All right — I'll try it on the boys."

They lie still in bed, their eyes round in the dark — and they *listen* . . .

I leave the door ajar so that they can see the light, as I come out. Half way down the stairs I can hear them whispering.

"Whit-*wheet!* Whit-*wheet!*" he d' zay . . .

I think I've got a winner . . .!

TAILPIECE

Coming-up to New Year's Day . . .
Time to clear-up, take stock — to make Resolutions . . .
Of *course* it's worth-while making resolutions — I'm the eternal 'start-afresh' man! Some of them stick — sometimes!
Listen . . .

I'll get one o' they diary-books
    like I did oncest afore!
I'll mark-in times as folks was barn —
    and wed — and dead. What's more —
the times t' git the presents
    and send 'em on their way.
Then this year, mostly all on 'em
    should get 'em — on the day!

I'll write-in folks I got to see.
    I'll work me way on droo —
and pencil-in the *seasonal* work
    as earns a bob or two.
I'll even make a sart o' list
    to stick to every day —
then I shain't sit about and smoke —
    and dream the time away.

I'll get up like I used to;
    'alf arter six or so —
and teake a turn along the leane.
    Rain, frost or fine, I'll gwo —
and tober-on and come back fresh
    as arn I used to be!
And then — I'll weake up Missus
    wi' a nice 'ot cup o' tea.

That way — we'll all be up on time.
    No squabblen round — no 'aste —
no breakfasts missed and nothen left —
    narn ov 'em ever late!
And when they'm gone, — we'll sit us down
    an' 'ave a quiet chat
'bout things both on us wants to do —
    and what next to be at.

We'll cogitate on garden
    and meake us out a plan.
I never *dunged* in autumn
    but there — I *will* do, — and
I'll set-in shallots early
    and *in time* the zeed I'll buy —
an' git they broad beans chimpen
    swo's they dun't catch the vly!

101

I'll cut down on me baccy. P'r'aps
    a pipe morn, noon and night.
I wun't gwo down the Malt House
    midday — well p'raps I might
teake 'alf a bitter. Or a pint.
    Well — p'raps not more 'n two!
Then — stead o' noddin' in the chair
    I'll *work* — the whole day through!

And then, each night come arter tea
    I'll 'ave *another* list
of things wants doen' round the 'ouse —
    swo's *nuthen* wun't be missed!
Nwo gawpen at the telly
    an' stayen up swo leate!
We'll be a-bed by ten o' clock!
    Well — *eleven* — at any rate!

That wun't the Missus, was it?
    Cawd lumme! Is that *snow?*
Looks starven-cold out there you . . .!
    I 'aven't *got* t' gwo . . .
"All right — all right! I *yeard* ye!"
    What was that she jes said?
Gone nine o' clock — Cawd lumme!

"O' *COURSE* I'M OUT O' BED!"

102

By the same Author

"VILLAGE GREEN"
by
Norman Goodland
(Price £2.50)

Other Books with a Countryside Atmosphere...

"THE VILLAGE SCHOOL"
by
ELIZABETH MERSON

"A HAMPSHIRE YEAR"
by
Noreen O'Dell

Published by Paul Cave Publications Ltd.,
74 Bedford Place, Southampton.